19.95

Mario Botta

Pierluigi Nicolin

Mario Botta

Buildings and projects 1961-1982

Electa/Rizzoli
NEW YORK

Translations
Christopher H. Evans
Richard Sadleir
Rodney Stringer

Photos
Alo Zanetta
except
Maria Botta Della Casa: p. 20
Daniel Leguerlier: pp. 20, 22
Remo Leuzinger: pp. 72, 118
Paolo Pedroli: pp. 19, 108, 113
Maurizio Pelli: pp. 43, 58

My thanks go to all who have helped and inspired me with their contributions to the critical reasoning which underlies my whole work; in particular my friends Tita Carloni, Lio Galfetti, Flora Ruchat and Luigi Snozzi, whose signatures appear together with mine on some of the projects presented here.
I would also like to thank all the many collaborators of my studio, both past and present, who have worked with me on these projects.

M.B.

First published in 1984 in the United States of America by
RIZZOLI INTERNATIONAL PUBLICATIONS, INC.
712 Fifth Avenue, New York, New York 10019
All rights reserved
No part of this book may be reproduced in any manner whatsoever without permission from Rizzoli International Publications, Inc.
© Copyright 1984
by Electa Editrice
Milano
LC: 83-42994
ISBN: 0-8478-0512-3
Printed in Italy

Contents

9 Note to the work of Mario Botta by Pierluigi Nicolin

Houses
16 Genestrerio
18 Stabio
20 Cadenazzo
22 Riva San Vitale
24 Manno
26 Ligornetto
30 Pregassona
34 Massagno
38 Viganello
42 Stabio
46 Origlio
52 Morbio Superiore

Buildings
56 Competition for a school in Locarno
58 Secondary school in Morbio Inferiore
66 Municipal gymnasium in Balerna
68 Library of the Capuchin monastery in Lugano
72 Transformation and re-use of a farmhouse at Ligrignano
74 Artisan center in Balerna
78 State Bank in Freiburg
86 Project for artisan building in Balerna
88 Competition for an administrative and reception building in Brühl
90 Project for a clinic in Agra
94 Project for the Guernica Museum in Guernica
96 Administrative and commercial building in Lugano
98 Maison de la Culture in Chambéry
102 Project for a building on the square of the T.G.V. station in Lyons
104 Project for the new offices of the Bank of Gothard in Lugano

Large-scale projects
108 Project for a master plan of the new Lausanne Polytechnic
112 Competition for the new administrative center in Perugia
114 Competition for a housing estate in Mendrisio
116 Competition for the enlargement of Zurich station
122 Competition for the redevelopment of an area in Basel
126 Project for a lake-side recreational area in Lugano
128 Competition for a science center in Berlin
130 Reintegration of the city center in Stuttgart

Design
134 Two chairs
137 Biographical note
139 Bibliography

Note to the work of Mario Botta
Pierluigi Nicolin

Language and construction
For a while it seemed as if those of Mario Botta's works that have actually been realized (within the limits of modest professional work opportunities) have lent substance to a range of imagery that was limited to the production of watercolors, axonometric and perspective drawings colored with crayons. For this reason his constructions, forcing a de facto recognition of their right to exist, have been very favorably received.
Not only did it appear that these works, taking their inspiration in part from drawings, justified their existence, but that the very fact of their having been built cleared the way for a confrontation with the reality of a world of figures that would otherwise have been doomed to remain on paper.
For a long time Botta has been perhaps the only one to have set down his cement bricks in between the handsome sheets of an architecture that exists only on the drawing board and the unsightly buildings of an architecture that has merely been constructed.
This is perhaps why he has found himself in a peculiar situation in recent years, a period in which the creators of paper architecture have been struggling with the difficulties of construction and thereby exposing themselves to the reactions of the professional world. As a consequence Botta the artisan architect has been torn to demonstrate the validity of both sides of the argument: that of the eclectic professionals with no talent and that of the artists with classical aspirations but no part to play.
An understanding of the special position his work occupies in the wider context of the present debate may be aided by a comparison of the comments which accompanied the publication of a book devoted entirely to his round house in Stabio. This small volume appeared in 1982 with a poetic introduction by Sanguineti.
In his own highly personal interpretation, Alberto Sartoris recognizes in this work the confirmation of Botta's status as an alchemist of geometry and describes the work itself as original invention in the universe of pure poetry. Thus "in virtue of the correspondence between ideas, principles and numbers" and regulatory plans, this ideographic cylinder is projected century after century into the "geometric splendor" of works of architecture which illustrate the symbolism and magic of the constructed circle. He closes his remarks by affirming that Botta "aims for and transposes the creative rigor of early Rationalism."
Rob Krier addresses himself to his artisan friend as an artist architect, prefacing his comments with a confession about the shortcomings of his own, rare, constructions. "For you everything is different. You can show off each of your buildings, inside as well as out. They are unharmed by their inhabitants and grow old gracefully. I still cannot work out how you manage to persuade a client to accept your ideas. Not only that, but they all seem to remain faithful to that idea of the house that you both preach and practice. I have always considered you a fortunate architect, for you very early gained possession of the qualities required to get across an idea of construction, and you continue to pursue your aims with extraordinary consistency. Equally important to the ideal portrait of a builder that I have sketched here is of course that tenacity in work and passion for the job which is typical of you."

But if architecture must be expressed in terms of types and rules then the symbolic content of this private home is out of place according to Krier, who would put it outside the bounds of what is normally understood by Rationalism, where unique and ambitious forms are reserved for the functions of public life.
Krier makes another set of comments on the relationship between the volume of the building and its openings. Basically he criticizes Botta for spurning the theme of windows for wide cavities in the bulk of the walls that allow the glass to be recessed behind the surface.
These apertures, he goes on to say in the book, are made at the expense of an unacceptable contradiction between the open display of a stratified system of construction, emphasizing the succession of different courses, and the way blocks are set in the concrete in correspondence with architraves and projections.
He sees this as a procedure that involves an undisguised abuse of the language of construction.
The comment by Reiser, expressed in the language of his cartoon strip, presents us with a "left-wing" key to the interpretation of this house that is not wholly extraneous to the foregoing arguments. Reiser's point of view is a decidedly fascinating one and of great interest when it comes to finding a place for Botta's work among present-day myths. It may also be a good place to start when trying to understand the reasons for his highly unusual success and the backing that his proposals receive from an ever larger public.
His drawings offer an interpretation of the Stabio house in terms of utopia and science fiction. As in science fiction stories, the *consecutio temporum* is overthrown, and the house falls out of the sky like a meteor or a spaceship, or even like the "holy house" of the Virgin which was brought by the angels to Loreto.
Once embedded in the ground it reveals its true nature: here we have an object with the allure of a mediaeval castle. But it has no problem in transforming itself once again into a solar house "which will have had lots of little ones by the year 2000."
The inhabitants of this house which has almost fallen on them from the sky will discover that it is nothing less than a synthesis of two classic archetypes of the dwelling: it is at one and the same time *tree* and *cave*.
As a tree it serves as shelter, a big umbrella that does not merely provide refuge from bad weather but leaves open the possibility of remaining immersed in the surrounding nature and scenery; its inhabitant is able to participate in the natural course of events: sun, rain, snow, clouds, spring, autumn, etc. As a cave it supplies the warmth and quiet of a maternal womb. Moreover the fluidity of space, lack of obstacles and free internal circulation favor the establishment of a domestic anti-Oedipean ideal.
In my own commentary I looked at the Stabio cylinder as one of the many family houses built by Botta in Ticino. I did this in order to draw attention to the recurrent features of a production which seems to me to be based on the idea of "varying repetition." Conscious of this aspect Botta himself sought to assemble a posteriori the plans of his houses into a single scheme that would show up their geometrical matrices.
A description made from this point of view, and based on the dozen or so one family houses built so far, would run more or less as follows:

A house by Mario Botta is:
— Three stories high; ground floor used as entrance, with space for a car if necessary, small service rooms, access to the stairwell; second floor with a two stories high living room, a kitchen and one other room (study, work, etc.); third floor housing the bedrooms and bathroom.
— Built out of unplastered breeze-blocks laid in the form of cavity walls on a concrete base and arranged in cunning textures of reinforced masonry, in correspondence with architraves and projections, made out of concrete and metal structural sections.
— Carved out of a simple primary volume, split on the north-south axis by a wide fissure closed at the north end by the volume of the stairs and open to the south through a broad glass partition that curves over onto the roof and lets light into the whole house.
— Without windows; they are replaced by a few large apertures deeply recessed into the volume of the house; these apertures can be transformed into conservatories by the addition of a glass wall in the outermost part.
— Without internal doors and therefore practically without real corridors; perhaps even without rooms, since the internal space is divided horizontally by floors that are open in several places, and the walls are set so that they do not reach as far as the ceiling.
— Well-constructed; the technique of using cavity walls made out of breeze-blocks, mastered to perfection, lends itself to ornamental adventures.
— Economical, since all the elements "on display" belong to the construction. The compact nature of the building and the absence of applied finishes also contribute to the low cost of this type of construction.
— An object in the landscape; it aspires to a direct rapport with the land, without fencing, garden or any sign of a limit to the property. The house sets up a resonance with the primary elements of the surrounding landscape (countryside, mountain or village profile, hillsides, sky) or with prominent architectural features (church, bell-tower, cupola, farmhouses).
Each of these houses is given a strong and autonomous shape that is related to differences in siting, the high "dialectical" tension set up with the chaotic suburban environment in which they are often found, the requirements of those who are going to live in the house and the formal solution which from time to time introduces new inventions into the formula that typifies these houses.
This procedure may perhaps be described in classical terms of the relationship between typology and morphology. Kenneth Frampton has likened the form of Botta's houses to Ticinese rural constructions, assigning the "vernacular shell" precedence over the interior "in a rationalist mould" and thereby involving Botta in a typically Venturian contradiction. But after our observations on the relationship between interior and exterior in these buildings, with their much closer ties to an ontology of construction and the principle of non-contradiction, it could be said — without apparent paradox — that his having stopped at Louis Kahn, taking from the American master not just a fundamentalist philosophy of architecture but also the sense of the relationship between form and structure, has allowed the young Botta consciously to let his buildings develop according to a constructive principle.

Even the controversial capital that links the circle of roofing in the house in Stabio with the outer curve of the staircase is assuredly a response to an architectural problem. It is more ornament than decoration. It is difficult even in this limiting case to find a genuine "second degree" exercise in architectural script: there is no deliberate detachment from the application, no parody or surreptitious quotation. Hence the fact that these buildings can accord with the logic of rural construction is not so much the result of a mistaken sense of the vernacular but due to their ingrained realism.

These observations could be of equal validity with regard to the spaces of the interior. These undoubtedly reflect the revolutions that have been staged by pioneers of modern architecture in the realm of domestic space (Le Corbusier is the first to spring to mind), above all insofar as these solutions, taking their inspiration from artisans' workshops or from artists' ateliers in a rejection of the bourgeois ethic, manifest an aspiration towards the authenticity of the world of work. Hence the justification for these solutions may legitimately be sought in the peasant tradition and in the streak of anarchism that has marked the intellectual and proletarian groups of Italian-speaking Switzerland ever since the 19th century. This libertarian and pluralistic reading (with the aid of Reiser's interpretation) can provide a clue to the meaning of these repetitions and differences that are a response "from the left" to the pluralism and fragmentation towards which contemporary European societies are moving.

The figure and the ground
Botta's work certainly has a sort of formal overload that marks it out, as if classical art's essential gesture of "standing out" against a background had been taken to an extreme.

This aspect leads us to Botta's unflagging criticism of a sociological approach to planning. In this his art "is the opposite of the sociological, philological and political sciences, which never cease to *integrate* what they have distinguished (they only separate the better to integrate)." (Roland Barthes, *R.B. par lui-même*). This art of taking a work out of its physical context is carried out by the intelligent use of a few recurrent figures or shapes.

For example the Roman theme of the Pantheon — the union of a *central space with a rectangular pronaos* — expressed with great clarity in the second artisanal center in Balerna (which remained at the planning stage) is repeated and varied in the library of the Capuchin Monastery in Lugano (an underground version of which is recapitulated in the competition project for the Picasso Museum in Guernica) and, handled with great ingenuity, in the project for the theater in Chambéry. In Lugano as in Chambéry the figure obtained from the prototype by the union of two autonomous spaces is the result of combining a central space with an existing linear building.

Corresponding to the linear organization of the plan in many projects is the figure of the *wall*. The faces of this wall are treated as unitary surfaces in which a single large opening is almost always cut. This is a recurrent theme in his residential houses, like those in Cadenazzo or Viganello (where there is a single large circular aperture in the facade, a direct derivation from Kahn) and in Ligornetto and Massagno.

In the larger-scale projects the continuity of the wall is preserved by substituting unbroken surfaces of glass bricks for the windows (as in the project for the head office of DOM in Brühl – Cologne) or sandwiching between two walls a longitudinal slit that carries light to the interior (as in the proposal for the new square of the train station in Lyons). In these last two examples the large central apertures cut across the building, transforming it into a portal; this advertizes the function in the case of the Brühl factory and acts as an entrance gate to the city in the train station square in Lyons.

The figures of portal, viaduct, tower (or pillar) are all, like the arch in tension or yet others, elements in Botta's method of composition, figures whose references in the panorama of contemporary architecture are familiar. What should be emphasized here is the recurrence of a few basic themes around which an entire project may be organized.

The town has offered Botta above all the theme and the figure of the *corner building*, with two urban projects in which the convex part of the corner, facing public space, is given prominence.

Prow or rock against which the currents of traffic divide, meeting-place, symbol of the alternatives offered by the urban network of roads and at the same time keystone of the construction of city blocks, this building pattern stands as a symbol of the 19th-century town.

In both the State Bank of Freiburg and the office building in Lugano the project is divided into three parts: the first two are made up of the wings, which are developed longitudinally according to repetitive architectural schemes; the third is formed by the pivot of rotation. These projects, both in 19th-century urban settings, tackle two recurrent themes in this urban model: the building at a crossroad and the building along a boulevard.

In the Freiburg bank the solution for the corner is achieved by the superimposition of the figure of a tree (a large glazed cylinder supported by a mushroom-shaped pillar) and the portal (cut out of the buildings flanking the two roads which meet at an acute angle). In the Lugano office building, set on a crossroad on an orthogonal grid, the volume is hollowed out to leave a square "pillar" standing at the vertex of the angle, a solution that recalls the house designed by Adolfo Natalini for the Römerberg center in Frankfurt. Like the house in Stabio, this building is based on a combination of the figures of tree and cave. In homage to Franco Purini, a real tree is set on top of the corner pillar, reiterating the presence of this figure. A row of trees appears on the roof of the bridge-shaped extension to the Zurich train station, and groups of trees planted in movable containers enliven the project for the reconstruction of the Rosshof in Basel. Architecturally arranged, they also form an essential part of the composition in the proposal for lake-side recreational facilities in Lugano.

Several recent projects have revived the alternative of *additive composition* previously adopted in the school in Morbio Inferiore, the project for terraced houses in Riva San Vitale and the artisanal center in Balerna (where four artisan-cum-residential units are united by a magnificent glass roof).

The residential units in the project for the geriatric clinic in Agra are treated as independent elements, arranged in a fan around the nucleus of central services, in a solution that recalls several concepts by Team X and in particular the Smithsons' idea of a "landcastle." A linear repetition of formal and functional units is also found in the recent project for the Bank of Gothard, this time with the declared intent of adapting the disproportionate scale imposed by the requirements of a Swiss bank to the street frontage of the suburban fabric of a town like Lugano. In describing Mario Botta's recent projects, extensive use has been made of metaphor. This may seem to contradict the idea that an ontological dimension of construction is reflected in his work.

The primary volumes of the buildings described are certainly not taciturn. But there is no trace of that concern with symptoms that calls for denaturing the prototype by some indication of the use to which it will be put. No irony or quotation in inverted commas can be found in these works, so redolent of history and the works of other contemporary architects. There is no blatant transgression of the relationship between form and construction. Even the appearance of ornamental efflorescences in some of the more recent buildings (one thinks of the house in Viganello or the last house in Morbio Superiore) can be seen as an attempt, given that a certain amount of mastery over construction has been attained, to lend "appeal" to a primary form; a variegation of surfaces that communes with the landscape in an impressionistic and pointillistic spirit.

But having cleared up these ambiguities, the overall metaphorical significance of the form of these buildings is quite another story.

The idea that the figure (the metaphor) is a deviation from what is considered normal primary expression is the dominant conviction as far as verbal language goes, even if this *classical* definition has provoked a *romantic* reaction which holds that all language is metaphorical.

As far as architecture is concerned, the question remains equally controversial, and this is perhaps why Mario Botta's work will continue being placed, according to circumstances, on one or the other side in the hotly debated argument over today's architecture.

Houses

1961-1963 **Parish house in Genestrerio, Switzerland**

When I designed this house I was eighteen years old.
What can I say about it today?
I remember the intense feelings,
I remember the desire to "create"
I remember the desire for "Architecture"
I remember the doubts and trepidations,
I remember the uncertainties,
I remember the certainties and the challenge of humility which this profession demands.
And also I remember the reading and the writing.
Max Frisch on architecture

...Everywhere the keen consciousness that what is important is not the created thing, at least not in the first place, but the creating. I would say: even where the value of the new will in any case be inferior, the creation of the new is nonetheless more important than the preservation of the old, whose significance is on the other hand not denied. To see how each historical epoch becomes aware of itself as the present, how it goes ahead unhesitatingly in order to be truly itself...
I see clearly that a building site is among the most pleasant work places in our time; it bears no comparison with the factory...
I did not know whether the architect's profession, assuming that I might be capable of practising it, would have had the virtue of restoring my relationship to the world, because everything was still on paper. What had driven me towards this profession was something else: it was what was not on paper; it was what could be grasped, worked with the hands; it was material form. Only the real practice of construction, the realisation of projects would have shown whether this attempt too had not failed...

From "Tagebuch 1946-1949" by Max Frisch

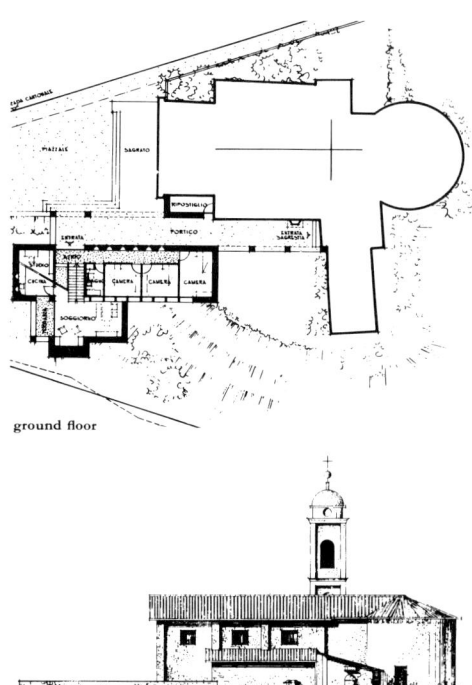
ground floor

1965-1966

A one-family house in Stabio, Switzerland

A flower for Le Corbusier

For a few months a young Ticinese Swiss had been in Venice studying architecture, while Le Corbusier was designing his last project, the new Venice Hospital. Mario Botta asked me if he could go to Paris. He wanted to work, even if only for a month or two, in the studio at Rue de Sèvres 35. He knew it was difficult, if not almost impossible. But he insisted and asked me to use my good offices.

During the summer of that year 1965, just as Le Corbusier's life was ending, Mario Botta worked next to Jullian and Oubrerie on the hospital project, in an improvised studio inside the Scuola di San Marco. And then, immediately after the Master's death on August 27 the young Ticinese left Venice for Paris.

...This house in Stabio, seen two years later, is the testimony of a genuine experience of life and culture; the deep sign of a spiritual memory, which for a young architect could only have been expressed by architectural reality; a simple flower on the plain of Mendrisiotto, which the great and superb Le Corbusier would have received with a touched smile and a quick broadside of questions, all contesting the legitimacy of the homage.

... And yet, the big wall which closes the garden and defines the whole habitat compared to the undifferentiated context of the countryside, the choice of the short side of the rectangle, and the restrained but highly tensed animation of the plastic masses, are the first, indisputable terms of a sound architectural statement sustained by its expressive dryness, its moral necessity and the defining capacity of each one of its spatial phrases. The items borrowed from Le Corbusier, such as the broad outside staircase, the fireplace, certain cuts to the walls, and even the formal slenderness of the two crutch pillars on the entrance front, do not detract from the poetic substance of this first architectural work. It is a pleasure to mention it in the present architectural season, so rich in formal experimentalism and theory and yet so poor in actual achievements, as a case apart, apparently to be discounted owing to its evident linguistic extraction, but in actual fact new and propositive due to the high quality of its expressed spatial image. The shrewd measurement of the lighting within would suffice to betoken an independent creative, remarkably inventive and imaginative presence.

... In this direction Mario Botta, a young Ticinese with a safe architectural vocation, develops his own critical intentions and expresses his own poetic aspirations, showing a belief in architecture as in one of the possible dimensions of morality, knowledge and fantasy. Along this same road the Como masters also passed many centuries ago, and they too were living in a time of crisis and violent ideological disputes.

Giuseppe Mazzariol, Venice 1967

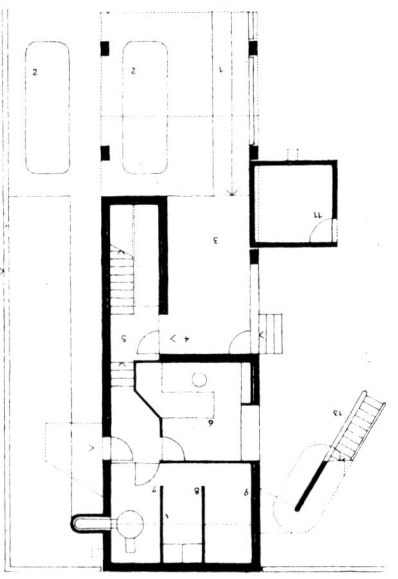

ground floor

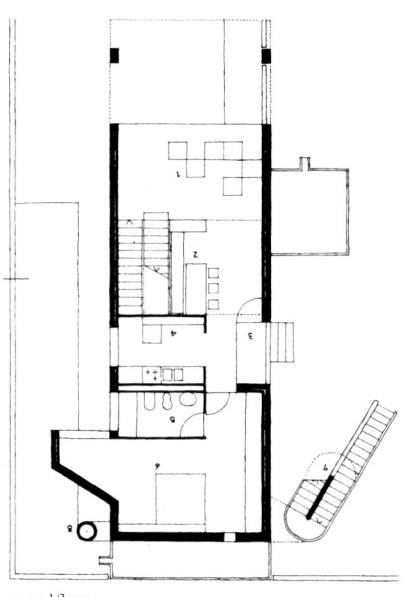

second floor

1970-1971

Family house in Cadenazzo, Switzerland

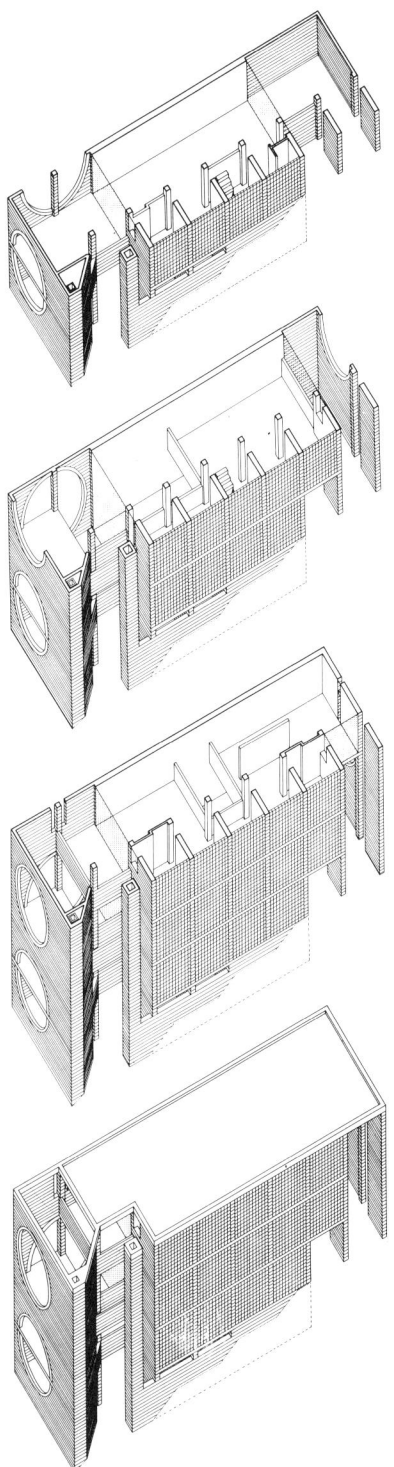

The building stands on the northern side of Monte Ceneri and looks over a broad plain extending from east to west, from Bellinzona as far as Lake Maggiore. In the front, looking south, the mountains delimit the horizon.
The site is surrounded by scattered residential buildings. This built fabric has replaced the old terracings on the hillside which used to be cultivated with vineyards. The building is set along the mountain slope, facing south-north from the upper to the lower part. The internal space is articulated in this direction and seeks to relate with the exterior solely along this axis. The construction to the east and west is completely closed, with no visual or spatial relation to the buildings around.
The space is divided on three levels. The ground floor level, besides the entrance, also contains the day area, including kitchen, pantry, dining room, living room and a broad veranda which extends the interior space and constitutes a filter of relations with the outside space on the north front. On the second floor is a studio with library and veranda directly communicating with the spaces beneath.
On the third floor are the bedrooms.
The dwelling is structured on the west side by a series of cellular services with cement-glass walls. A blade of masonry along the east front completes the static structure. All the masonry is exposed cement bricks on the outside and painted directly in white on the inside. The floors are reinforced concrete. The door and window frames are painted black iron sections. The flooring of the ground floor is black slate slabs.

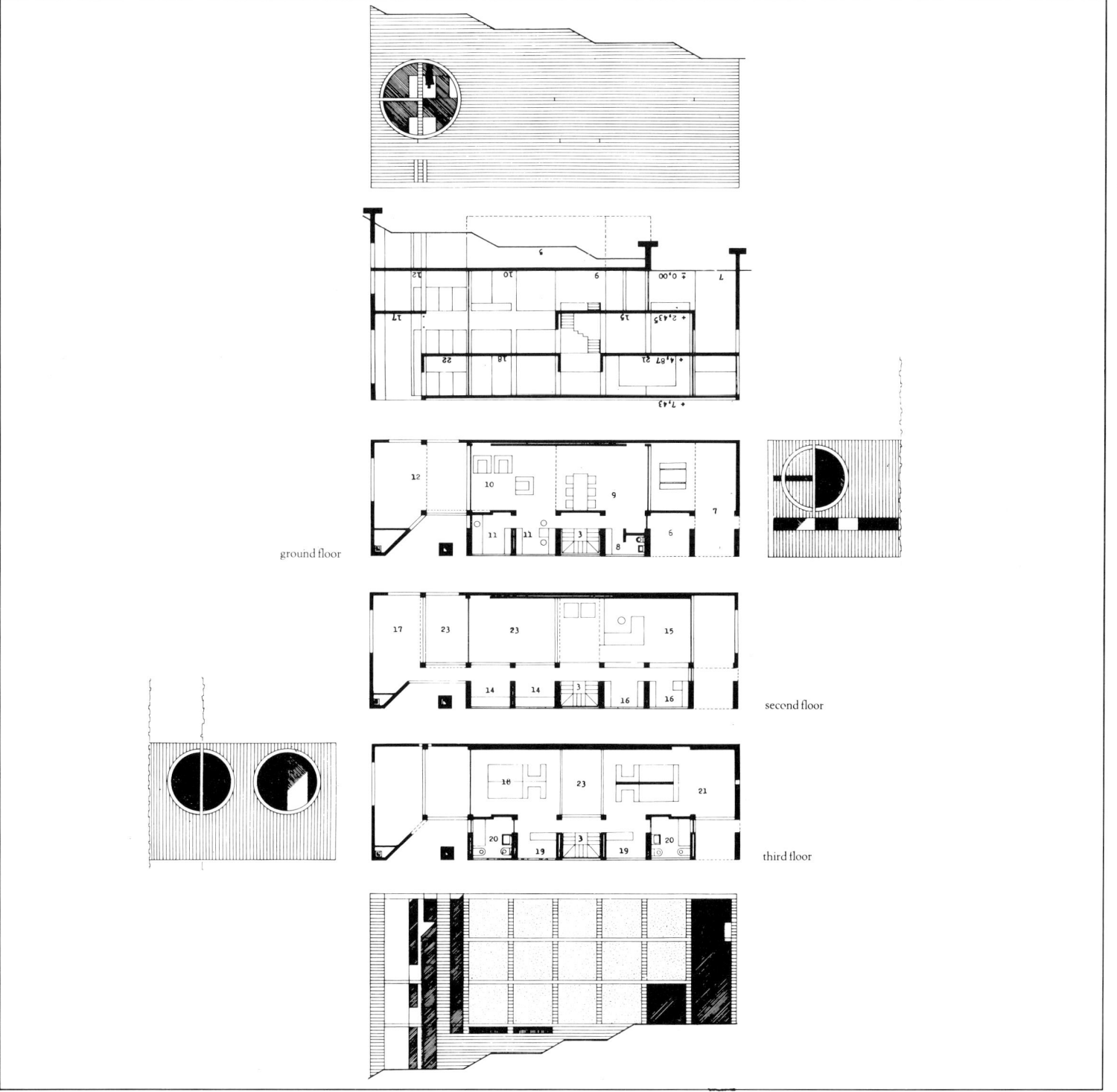

1972-1973   **Family house in Riva San Vitale, Switzerland**

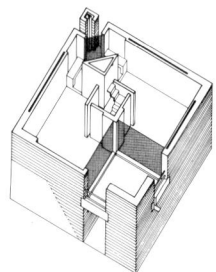
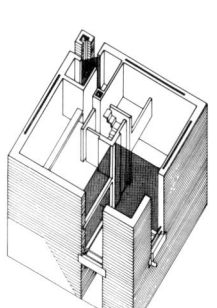
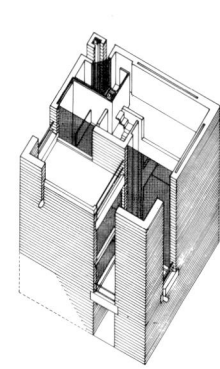

The building is on the shore of Lake Lugano, at the foot of Monte San Giorgio.
The site lies to the north of the old village center, on the edge of a village road which runs along the mountain slope. Beyond this road, to the north, stretches a wood which delineates the horizon. In front of the site, beyond the lake, the stupendous heights of Monte Generoso rise to the east. The new building was set in the lower part of the plot and laid out on different levels like a "tower," so as to establish a dialectic relation between the house and its orographic context. The primary configuration of this "tower" is solely virtual and defined by the structures of the corners bearing the roof slab. A spatial interpenetration between the inside and the outside defines a number of terraces articulated on different levels. These spaces are treated less as extensions of the house than as "filters" relating the interior to the geography of the surrounding landscape.
The constructional system, with bearing walls in light, unfaced cement bricks, without plaster and painted white only on the inside, includes reinforced concrete floor slabs. The iron section frames are painted black. The iron trellis for the entrance footbridge is painted red. The terracotta tiled floors are red. The whole house is built with "poor" materials, in an attempt to enhance their qualities and structure.

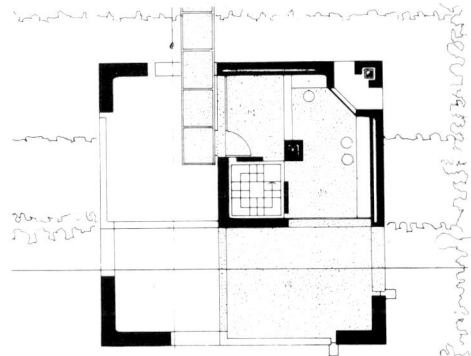
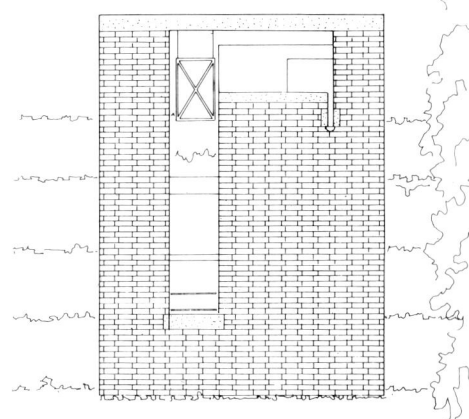
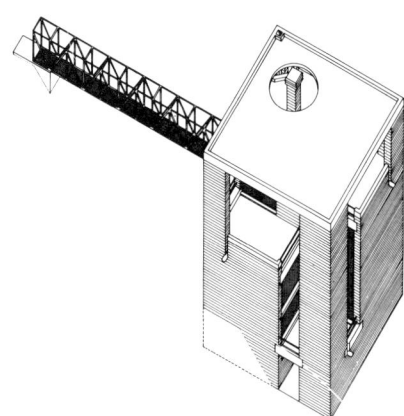

+ 3,89
-2,46
- 4,92
- 7,38
- 8,94

+ 3,89
± 0,00
- 2,46
- 7,38
-9,84

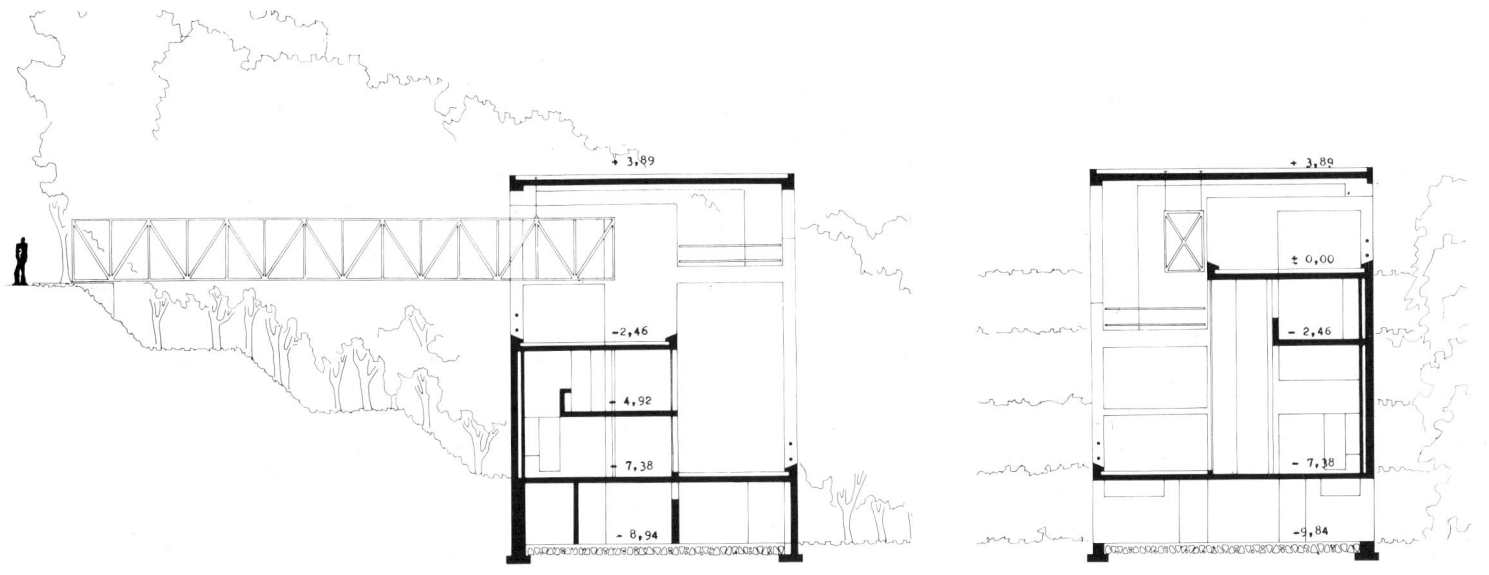

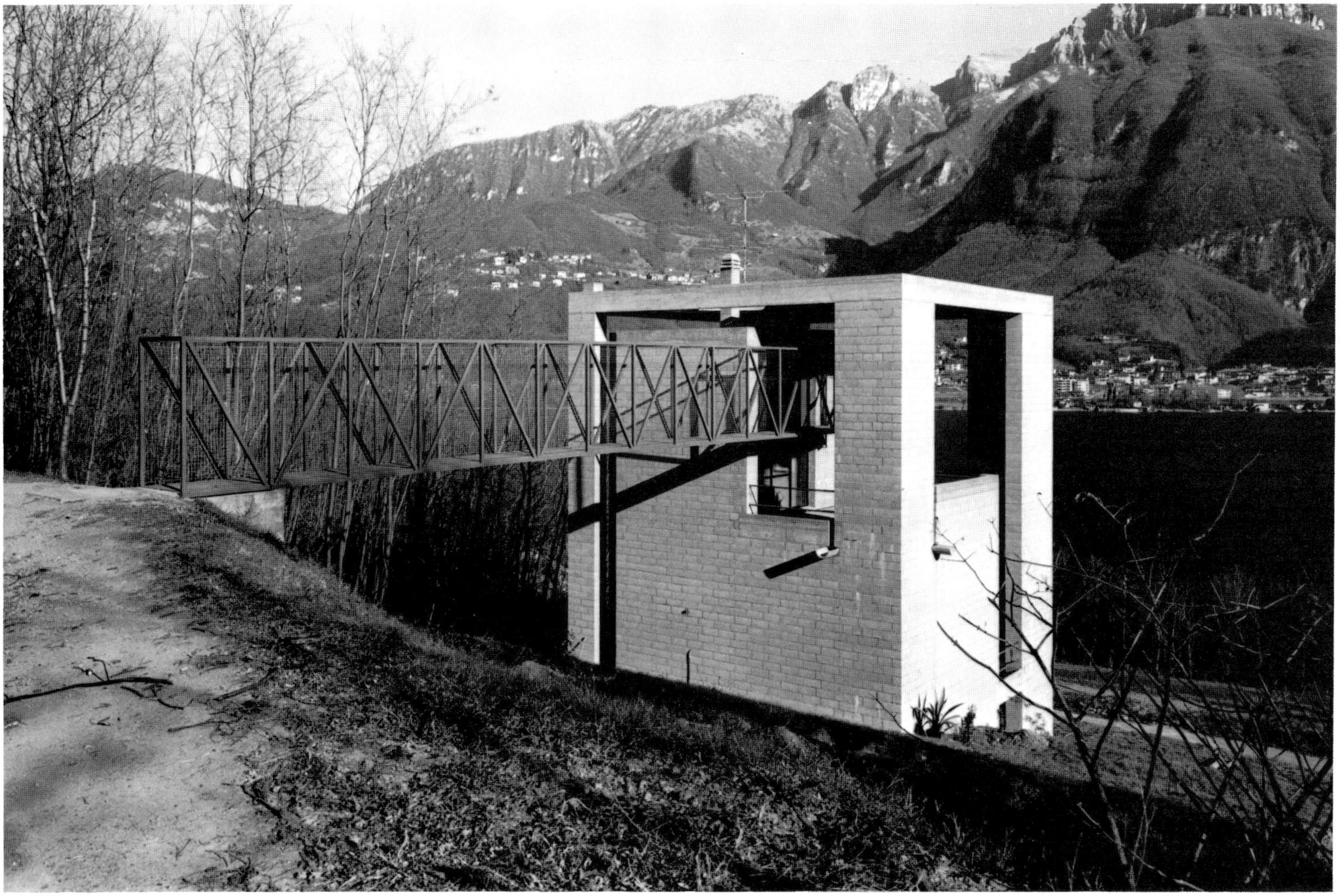

1975　　Project for a family house in Manno, Switzerland

The site lies at the bottom of the mountain on a slope facing eastwards, on the edge of a plain which opens southwards towards the lake and is not far from the old village center. To the south and on the upper, west side, it is delimited by a road which runs along the slope and connects the different villages. A little way above a large wooded area rises towards the mountain-sides. The house is set on the north-east corner of the land. The project envisages a line of poplars along the upper boundary of the plot. On the lower side, along the access drive, a wall spatially controls the large garden. The construction is composed of two elements:
— A wall-facade to the south, characterized by a big arch which acts as a filter between the external and the internal space. Around the arch flow all the activities, spaces and openings of the house.
— A continuous wall on the north corner, which wraps and defines the limit of the building vis-à-vis its surroundings. This wall houses services, stairways, fireplaces, etc.

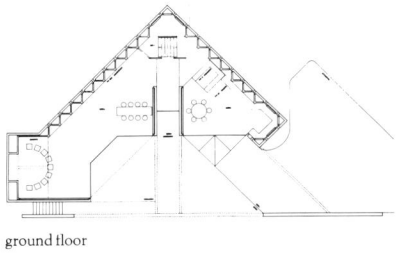
ground floor

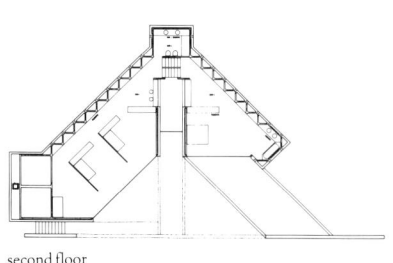
second floor

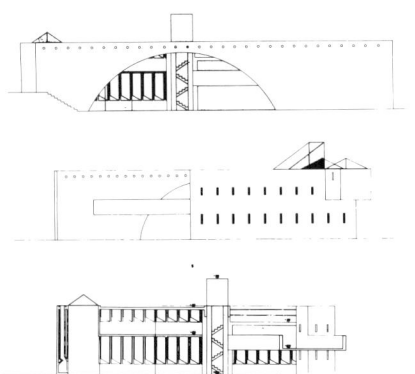

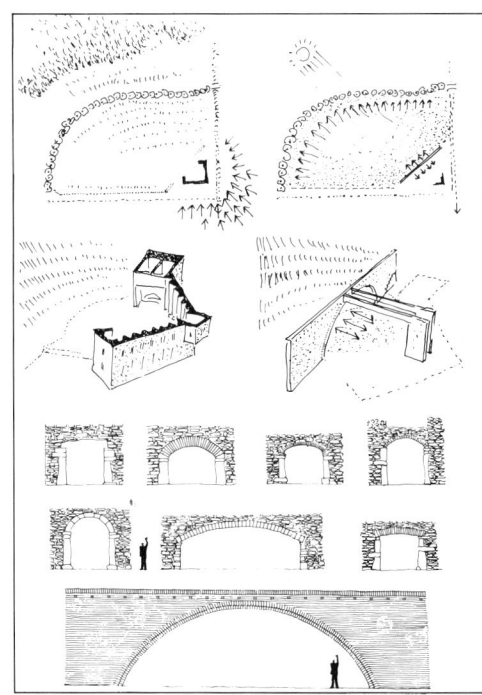

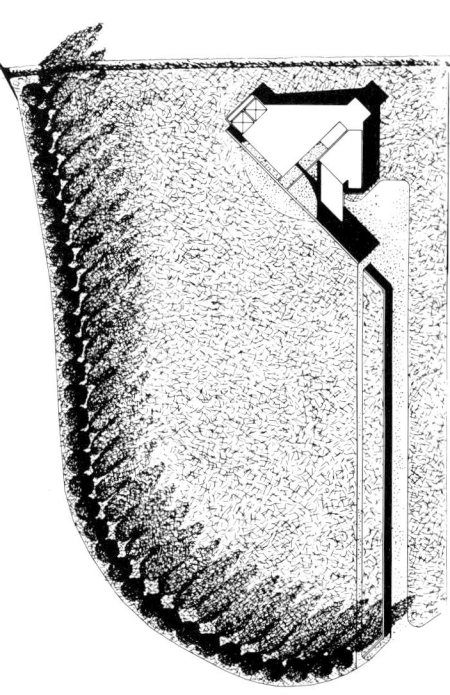

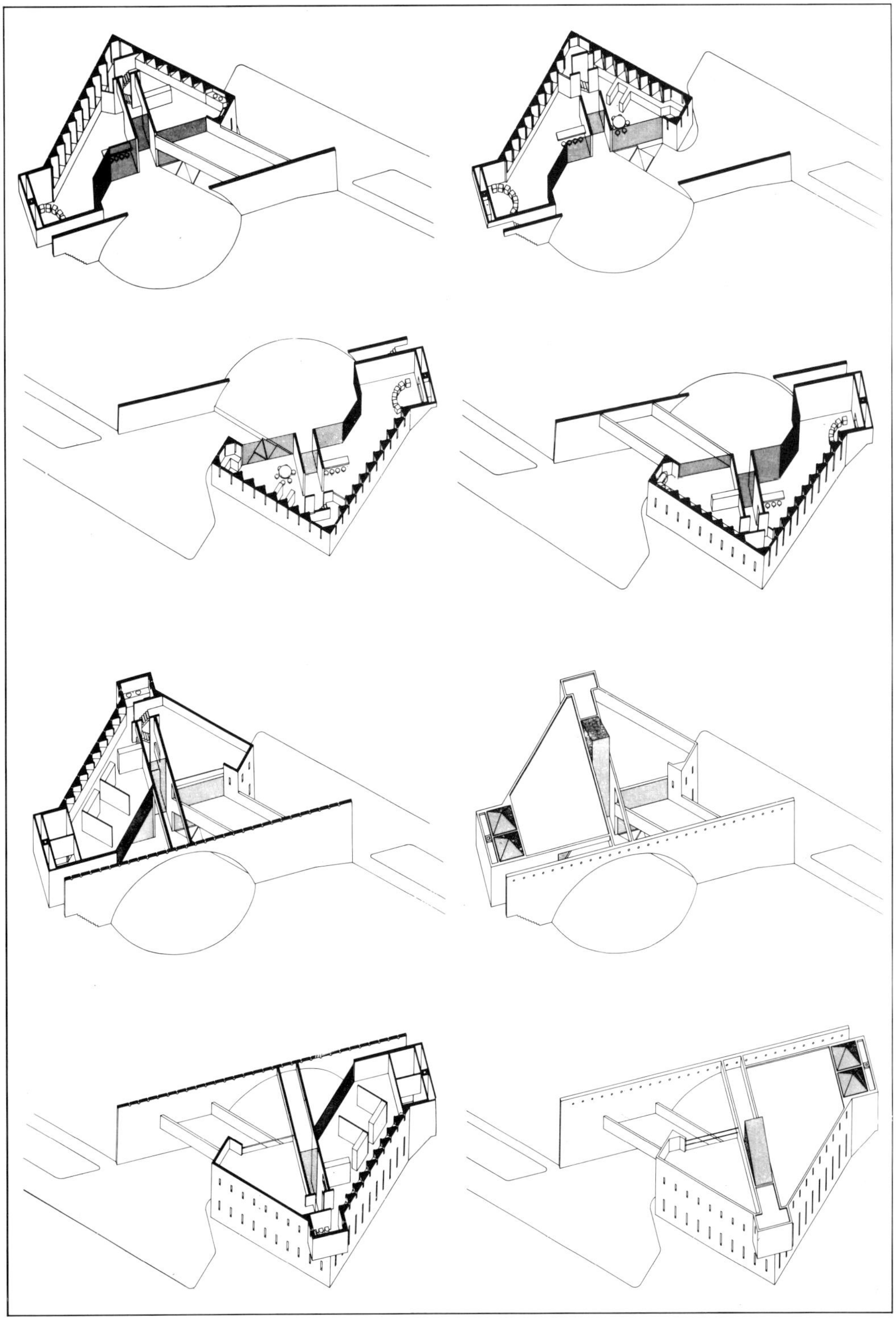

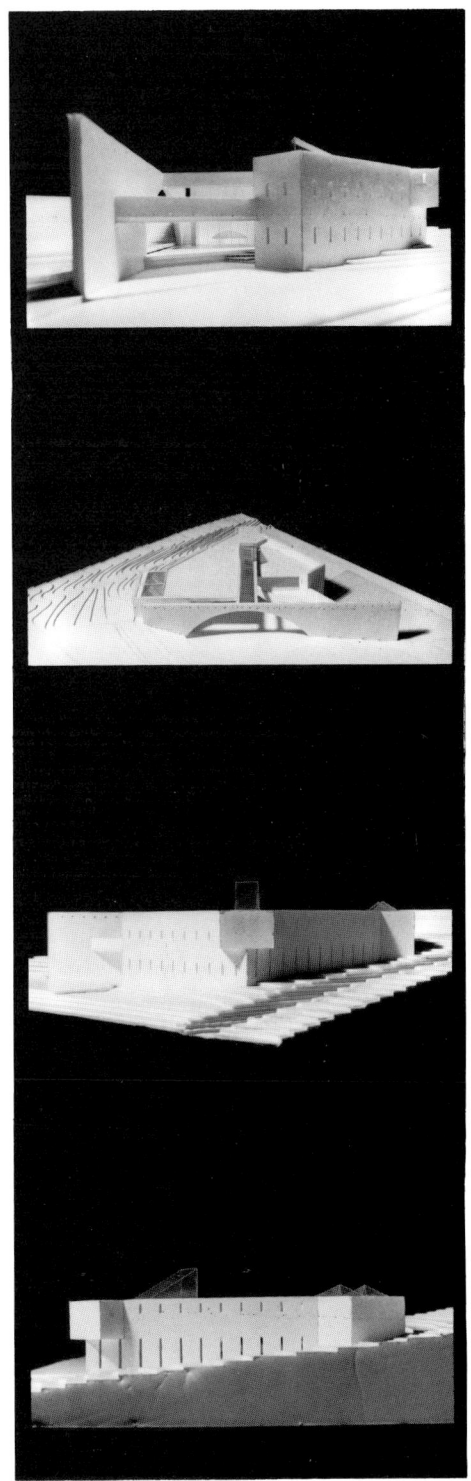

1975-1976

Family house in Ligornetto, Switzerland

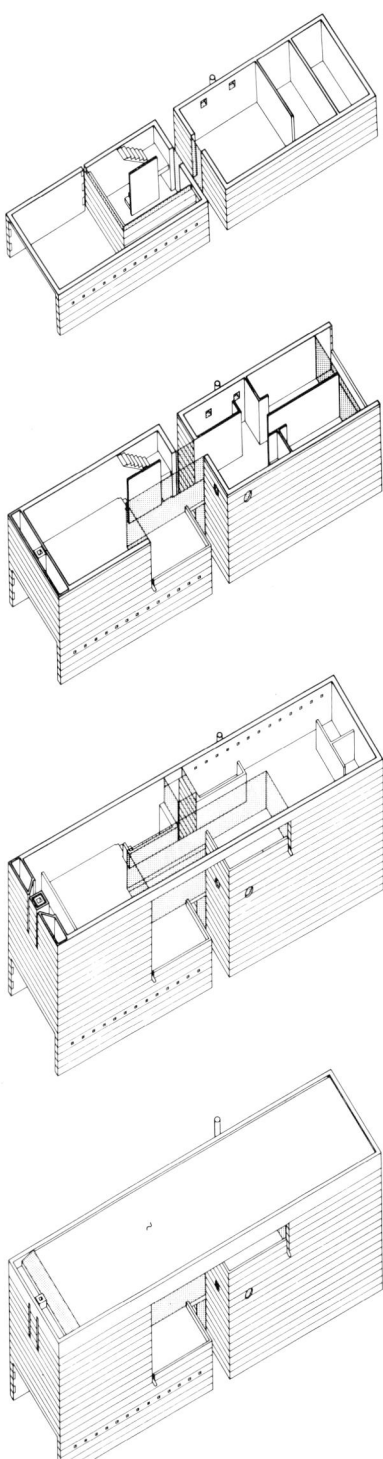

The site lies on the outskirts of the old village, among residential buildings along the roadway. This development mostly consists of detached family dwellings built on old agricultural plots. The internal roads serving these building lots follow the pattern of the original farm paths. The house is situated along the north side of the plot, longitudinally to the boundary; it also marks the limit of building development allowed for the village. Beyond that limit stretches the countryside. The desire for a clear relationship between the new built area and the remaining countryside formed the basis of this project. A flat front (the north facade) expresses this desire for a "limit" between the urban agglomeration and the agricultural landscape around it. The horizontal striped treatment of the facades is intended to emphasize the "artificial," designed appearance of the new building as opposed to its surrounding scenery.

This theme of "designing" facades is to be found in the local architectural tradition. It is a mark of the people's attention, care and love for their habitat, in a very severe constructional tradition in keeping with the primary requirements of living. It is a sign of poor people's "wealth."

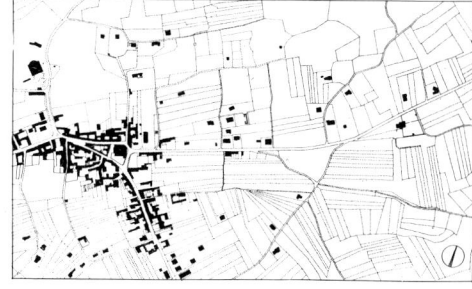

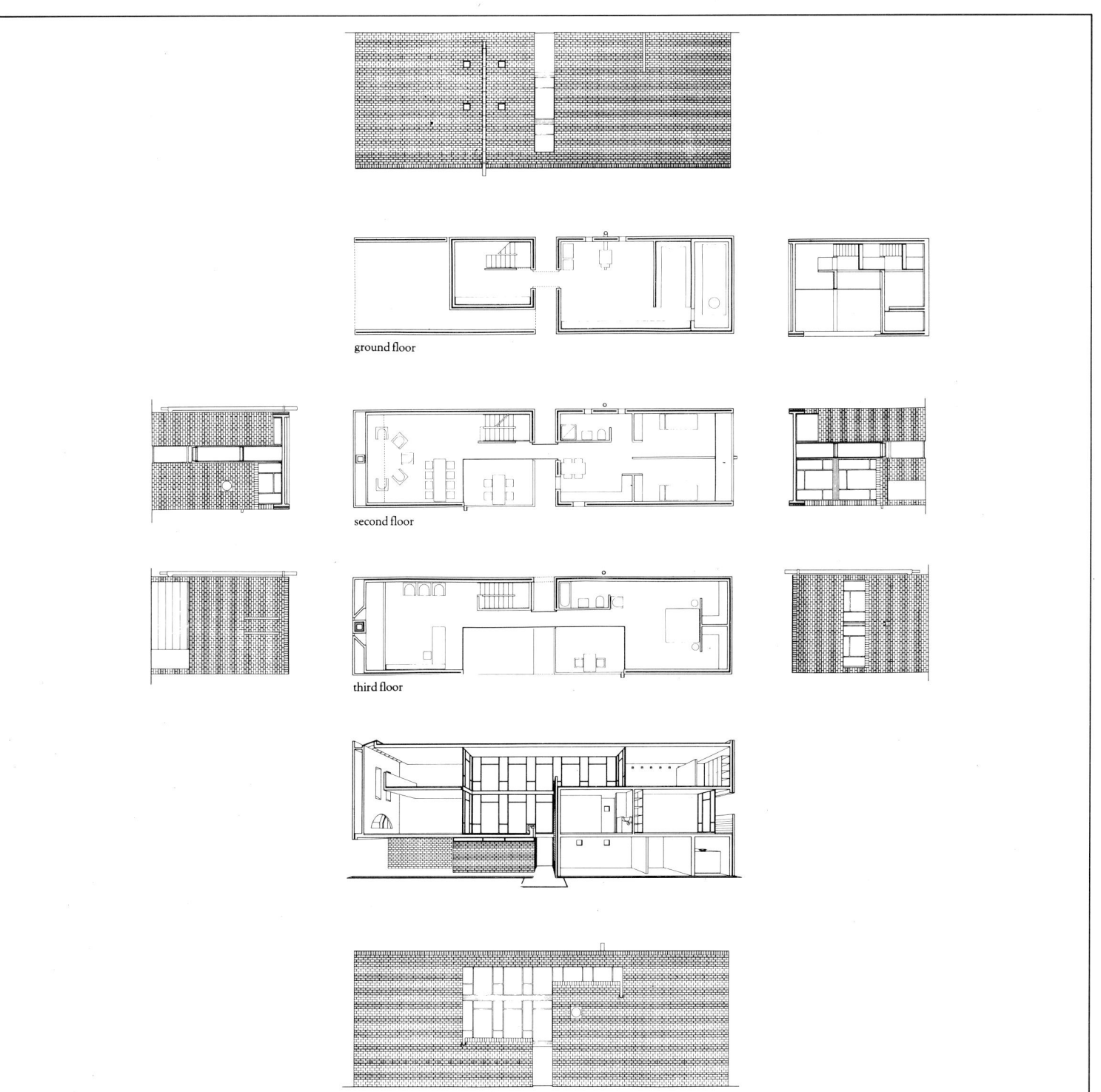

1979

Family house in Pregassona, Switzerland

Cut away on the south side and arranged along a central axis, the cube divides required activities on three principal levels. The entrance area is on the ground floor with two wide porticos, the daytime area is on the second floor with a dual system of openings to the east-west and south, and the night-time section in on the third floor with two triangular terraces on the east and west sides.
The apertures cut deeply into the central parts of the volume and draw attention to the masonry corners that enclose and recombine into the quadrilateral plan on the roof.

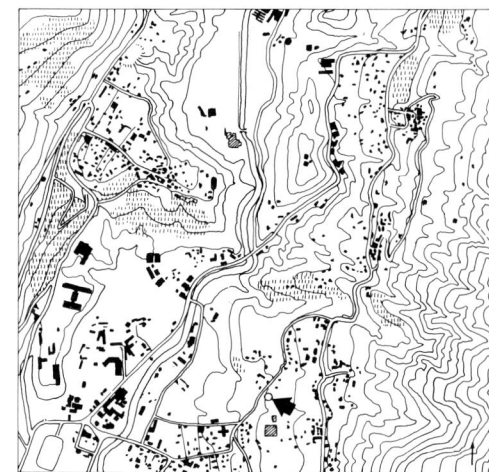

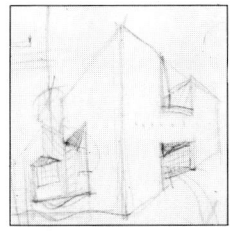 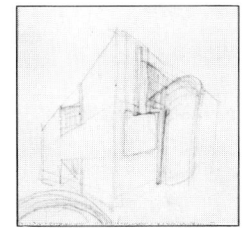 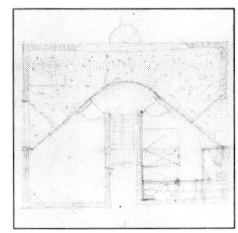 

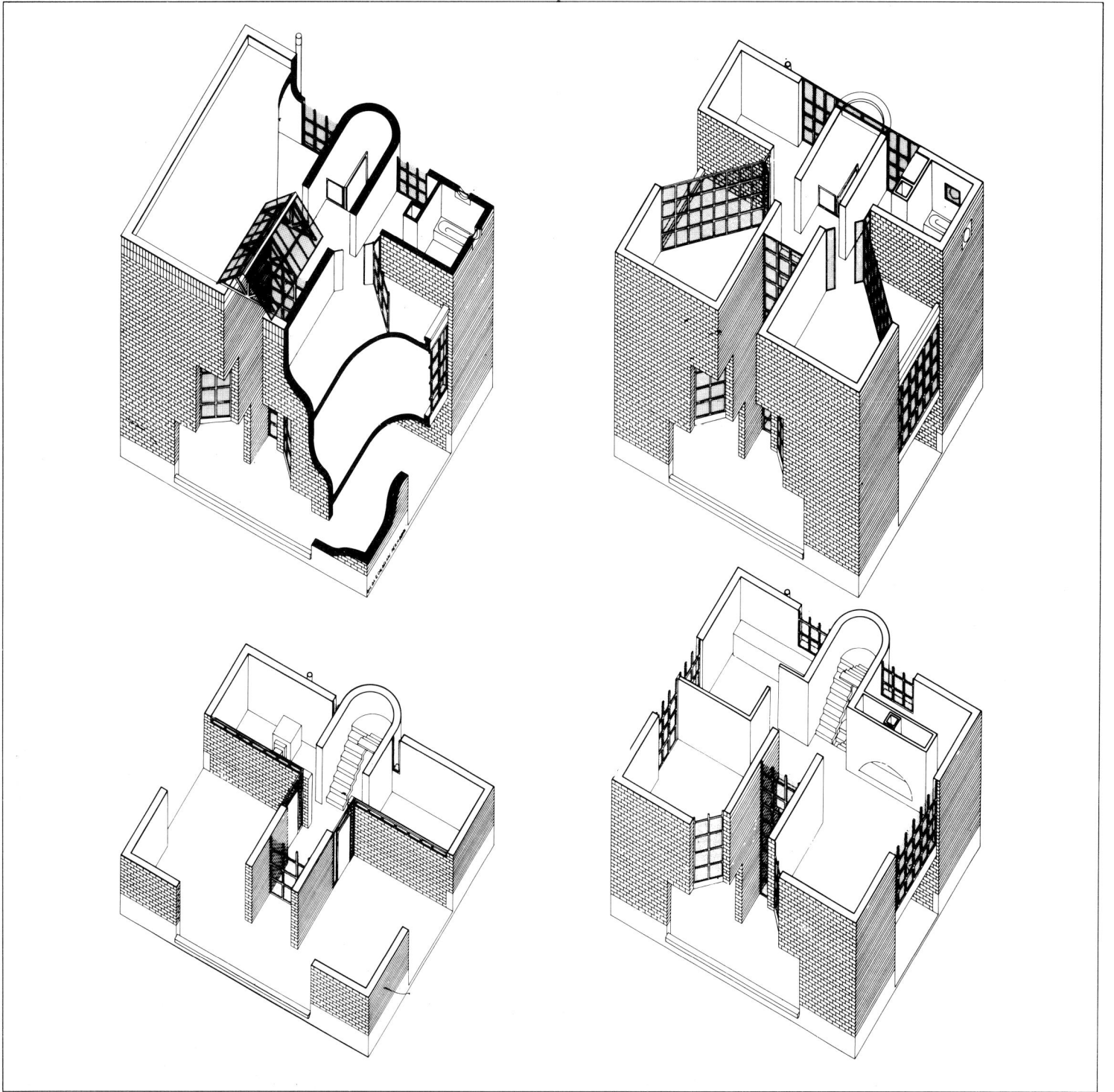

1979   **Family house in Massagno, Switzerland**

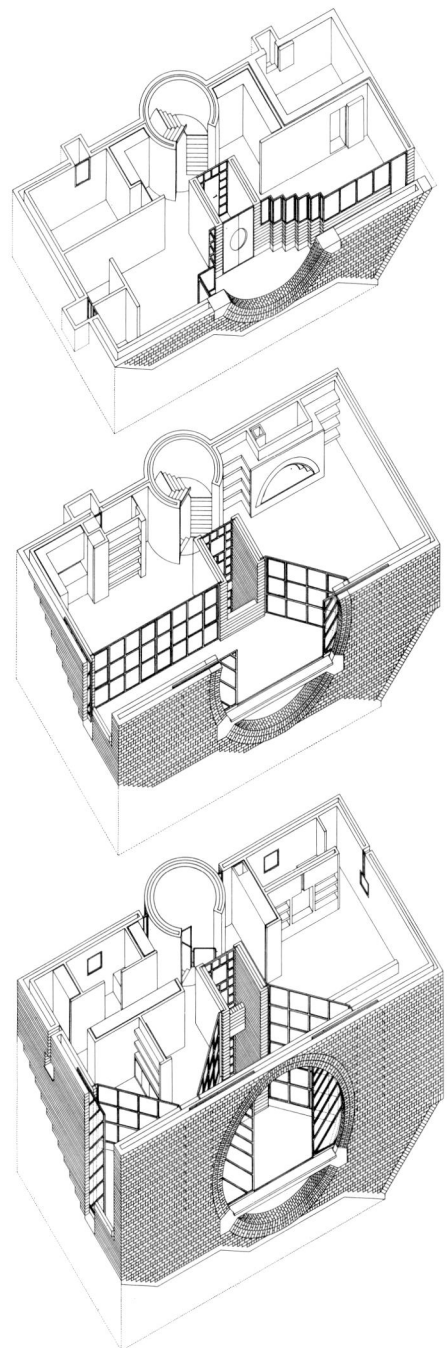

North of the town of Lugano and set on a steep slope facing east, the house presents a single main facade towards the valley. A broad round aperture on the central axis reunites the different activities of the three levels of the house. In this way life is oriented and projected towards the town below. The axis is also the source of light for the internal rooms thanks to two overhead points of light, one set at the center between two wall projections, the other set back above the stairwell. A system of sliding glass partitions allows the terraces to be transformed into a conservatory.

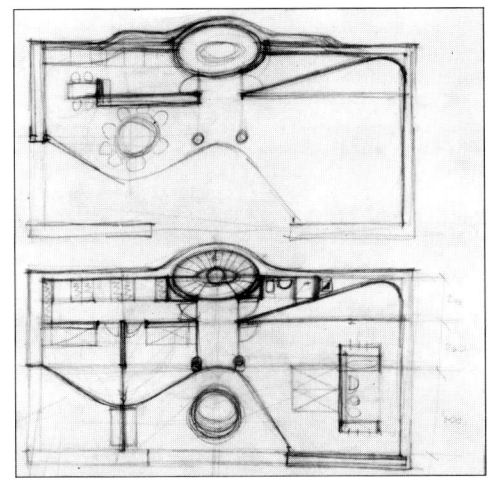

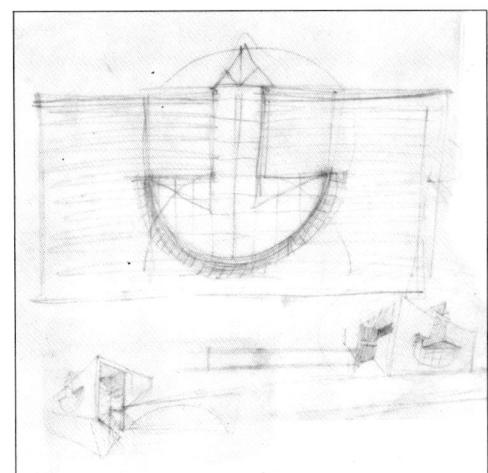

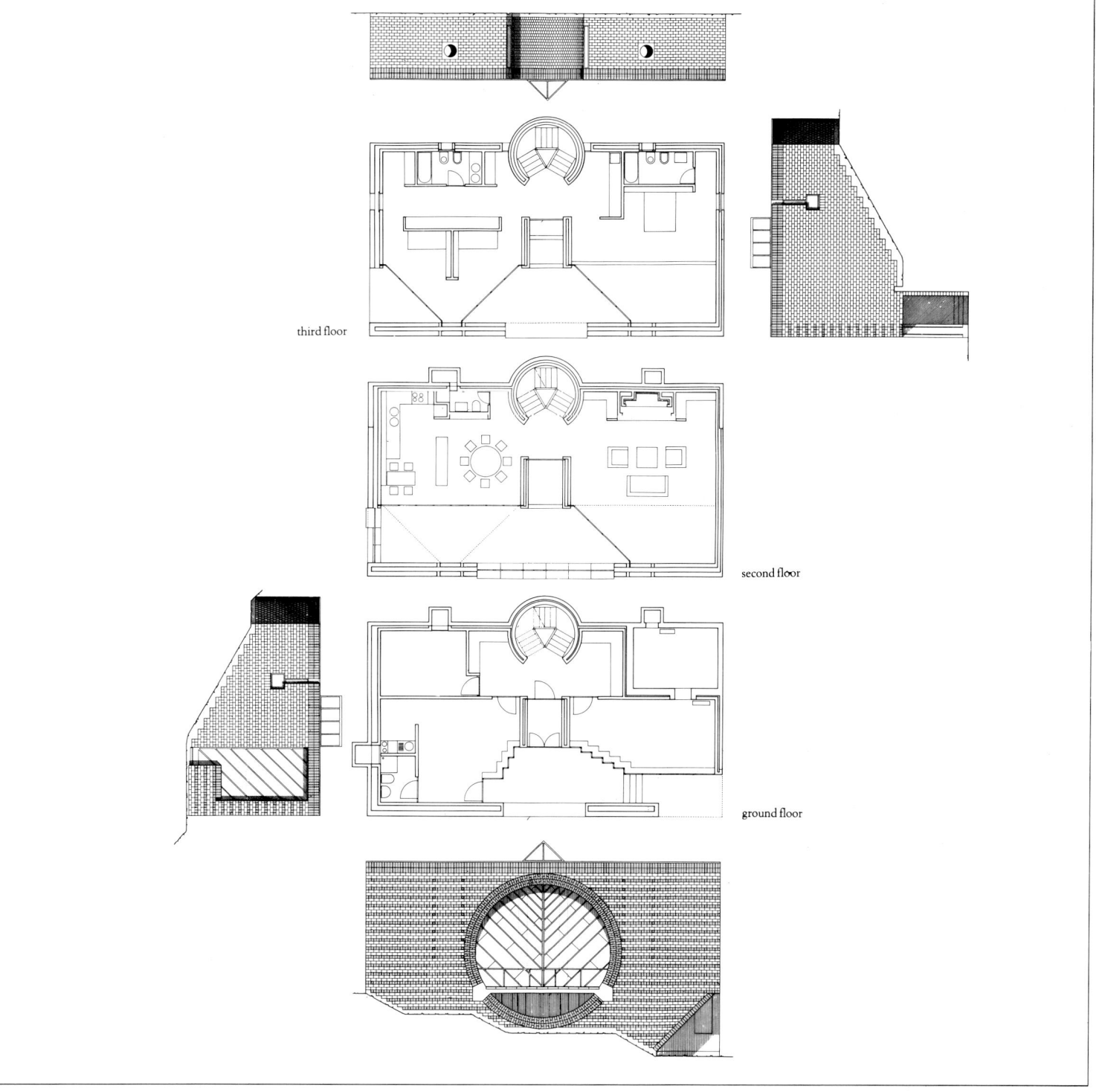

1980   Family house in Viganello, Switzerland

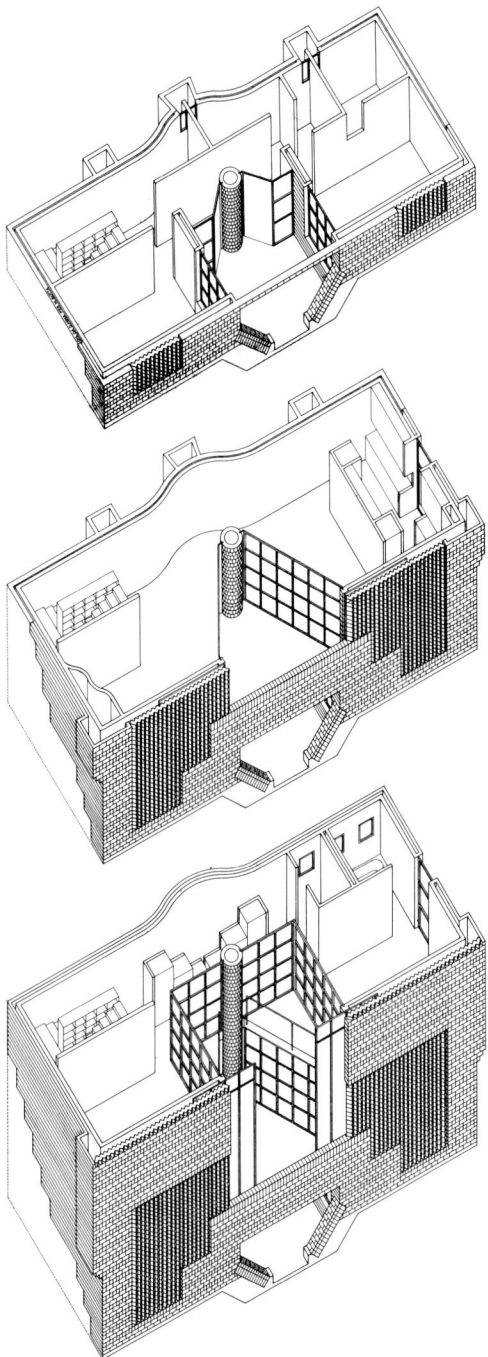

A steeply sloping site facing west determines the single facade of this house on the downhill side. The basic motif around which the project has been developed is the effort of taking possession of the land and the opening of the sky, the feeling of protection sought for in the interior and the striving for projection towards the openness of the exterior and landscape. The theme of the facade describes and narrates the interior spaces and its organization.

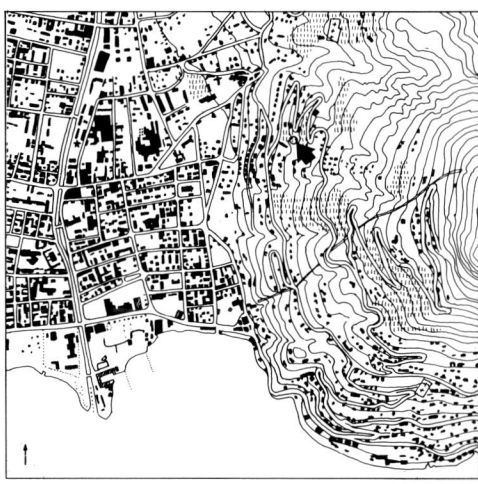

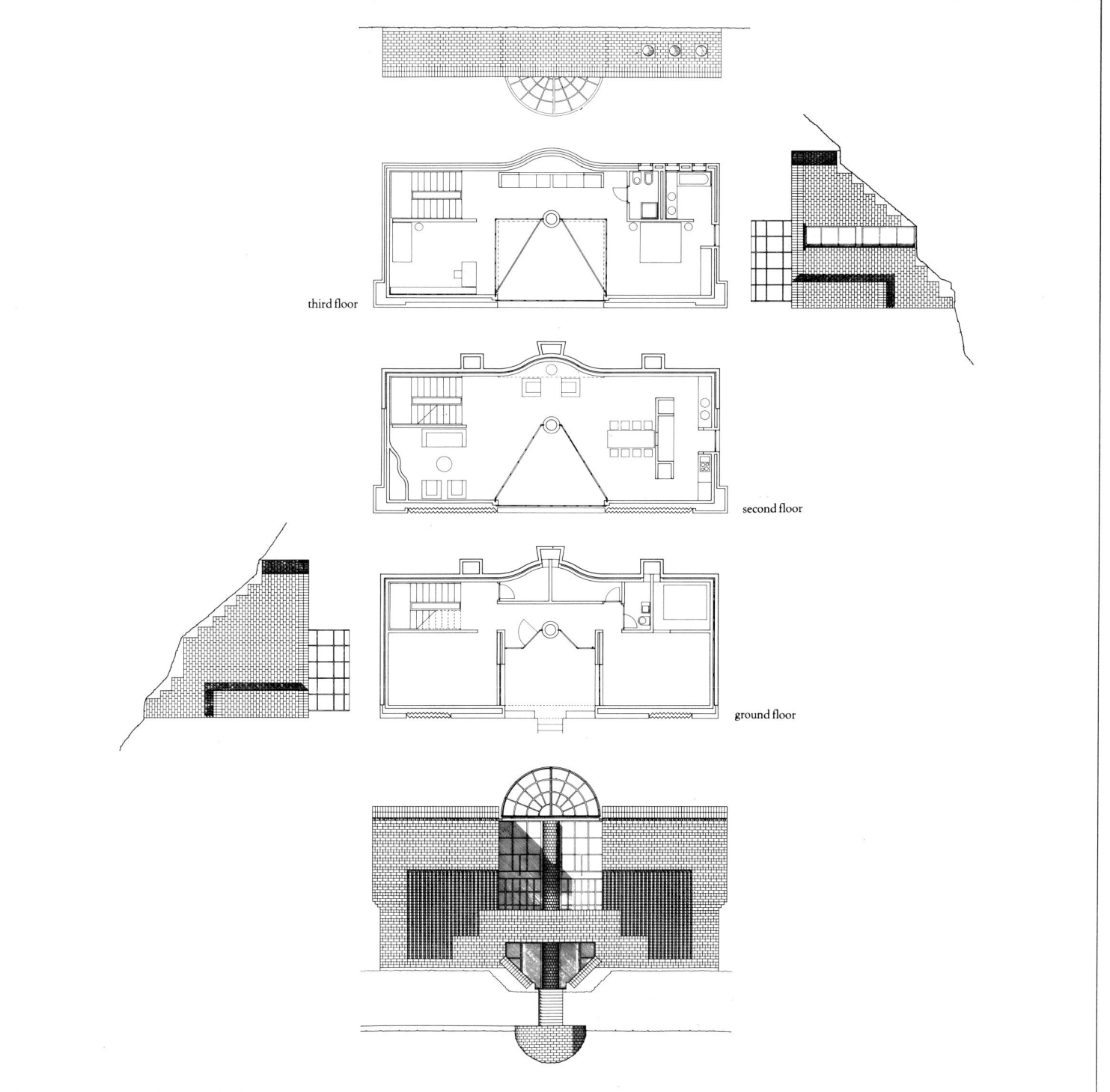

1980 — Family house in Stabio, Switzerland

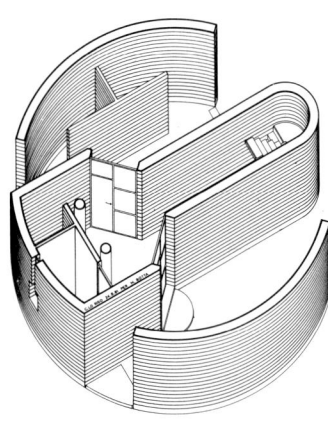

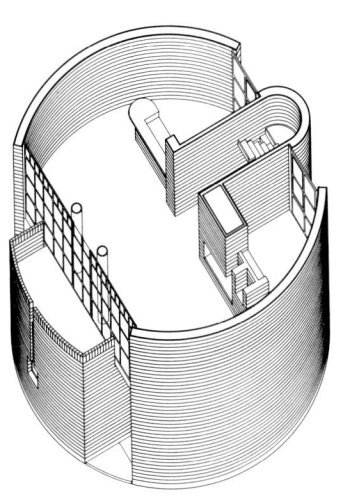

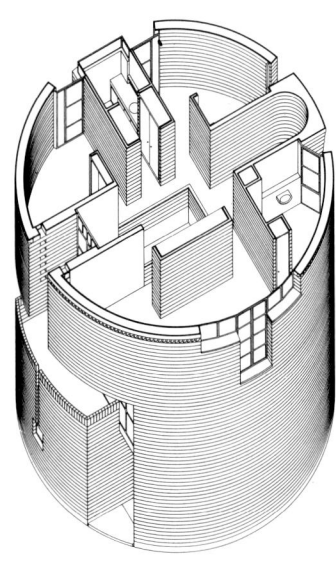

It is a circular building, cleft along its north-south axis by an opening that lets light penetrate inside from above. The intention was to avoid comparison or contrast of the building with the surrounding structures and to establish a spatial rapport with the landscape and the distant horizon. The house is a hint of a tower, an object that defines and outlines itself. The cylindrical volume avoids the need of facades which would have entailed a confrontation with neighboring houses. Such construction is rationalized by the space it occupies between the earth (to which it is anchored at its perimeter) and the sky (to which it is open vertically through its lantern).

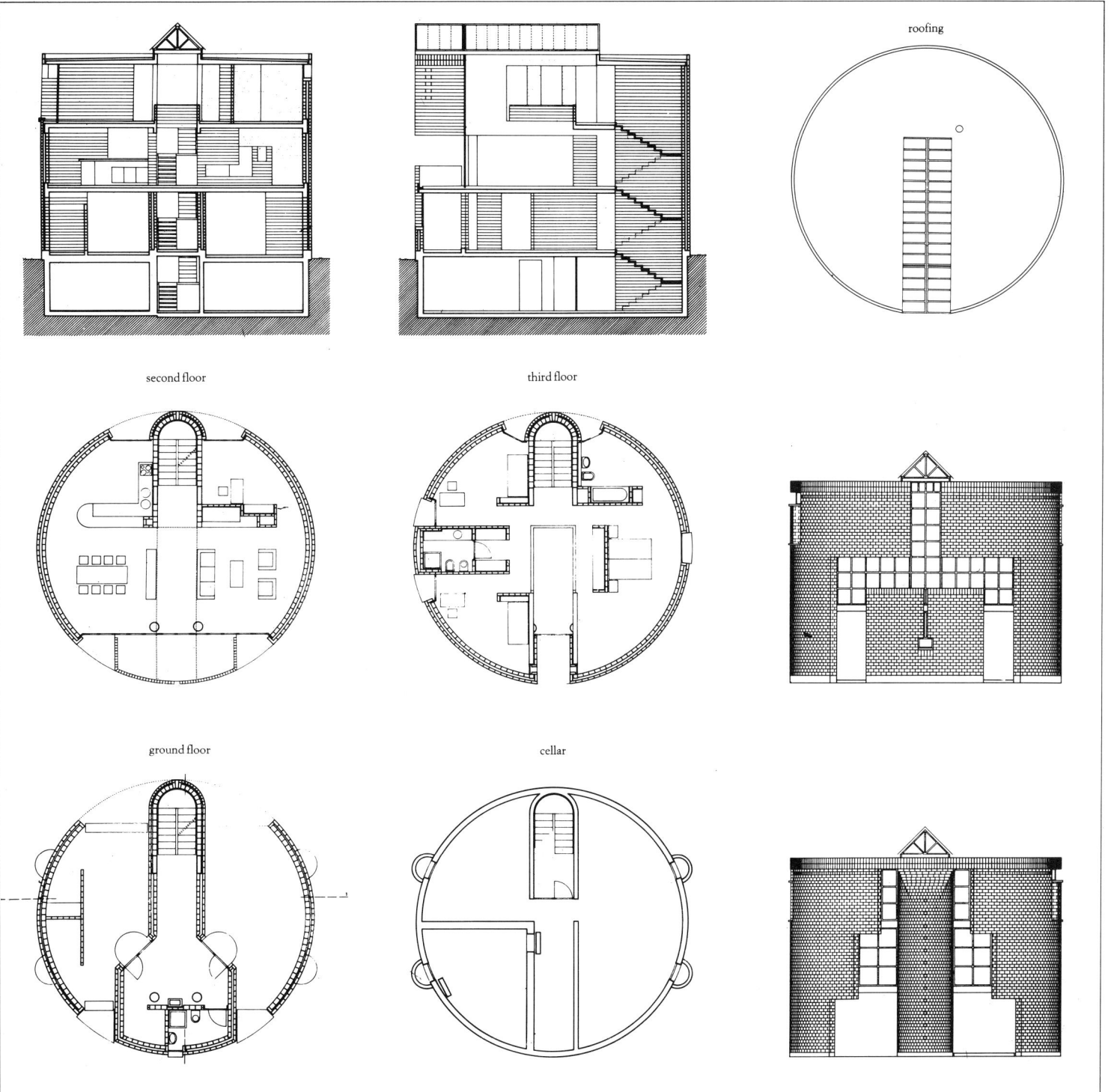

1981   Family house in Origlio, Switzerland

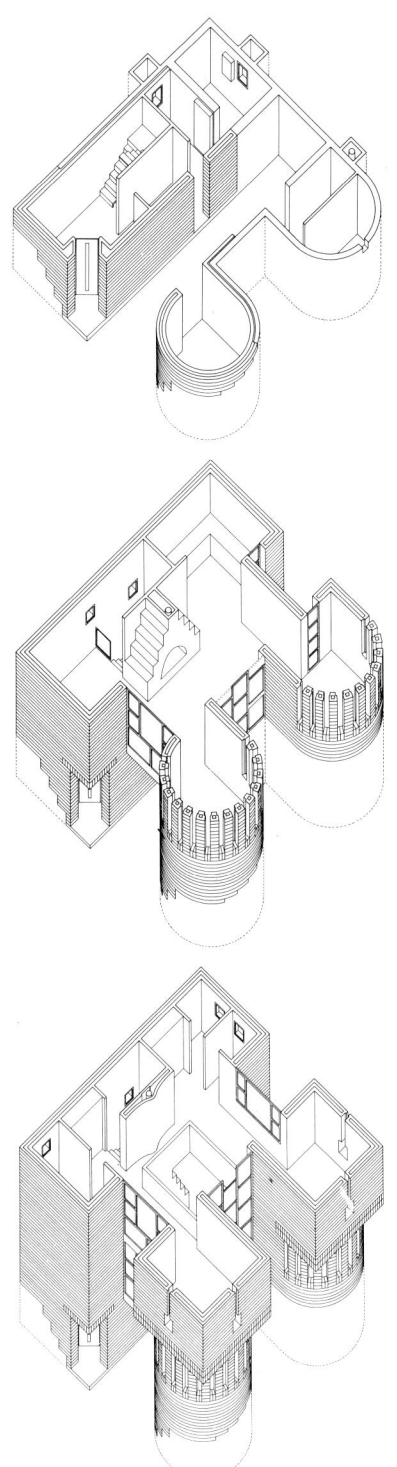

The living area is at the center of the planimetric composition and acts as a pivot for the different activities.
The volume is at the convergence of two perpendicular axes that point towards the valley in the west and the garden in the south, the two preferential directions for the openings of inner rooms.
On the second floor there are two work places, a living and dining area and a kitchen. On the third floor, the south side corners enclose the bedrooms.

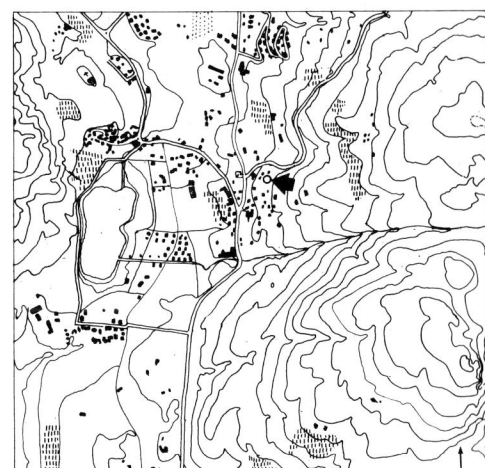

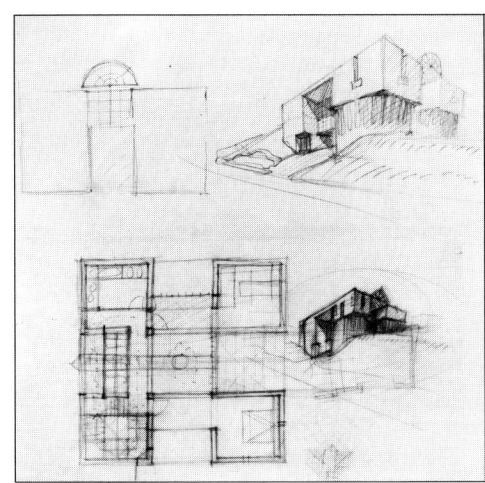

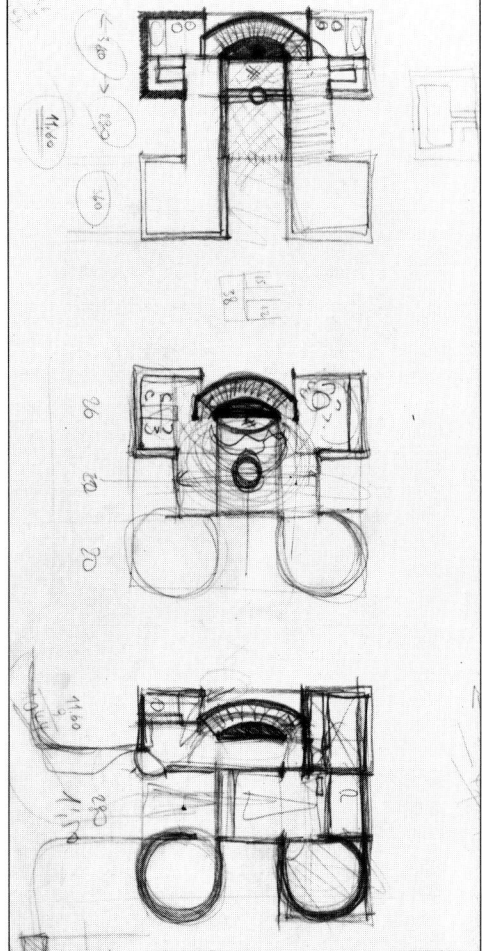

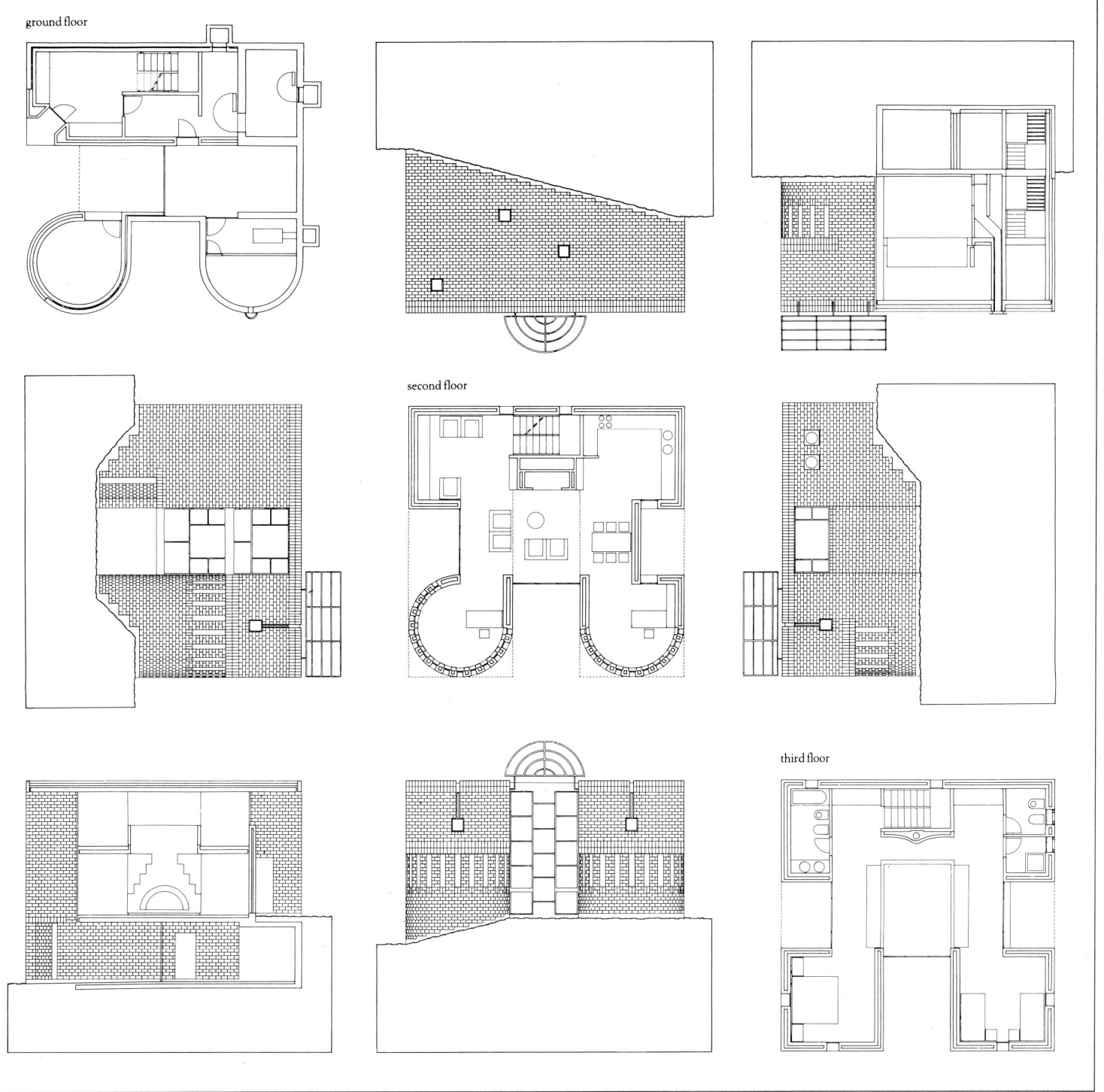

1982 **Family house in Morbio Superiore, Switzerland**

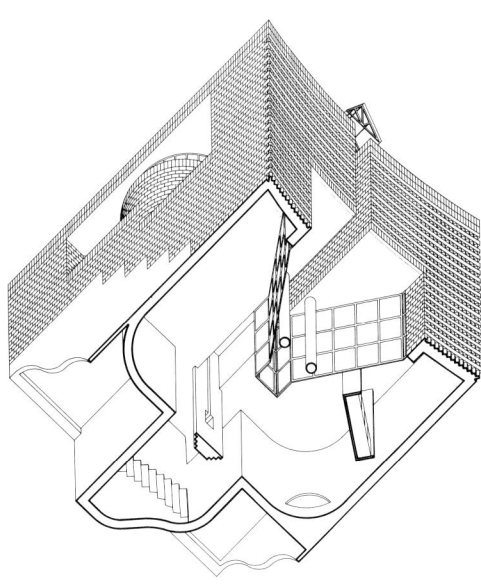

The house is set on a mountain ridge above the Chiasso plain. The construction originates from the typological organization of its special geographical situation. The house is between a flat terrain slewed towards the village in the east, and a steep slope facing the plain in the west. Uphill, the entry and the bedroom level rise above ground. The lower level on the downhill side contains the living area and related spaces. The two main levels are lit from above by a skylight on the east-west axis. The main elevation is slightly concave and frames the landscape.

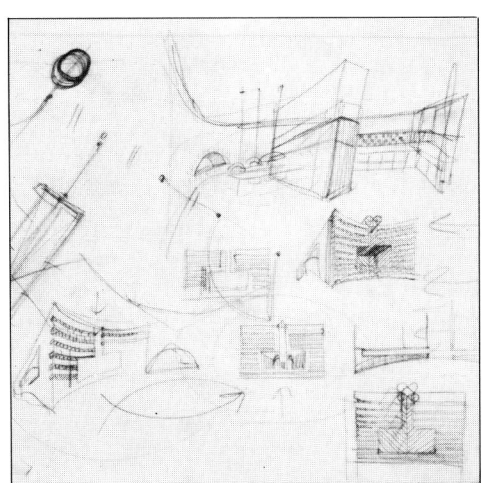

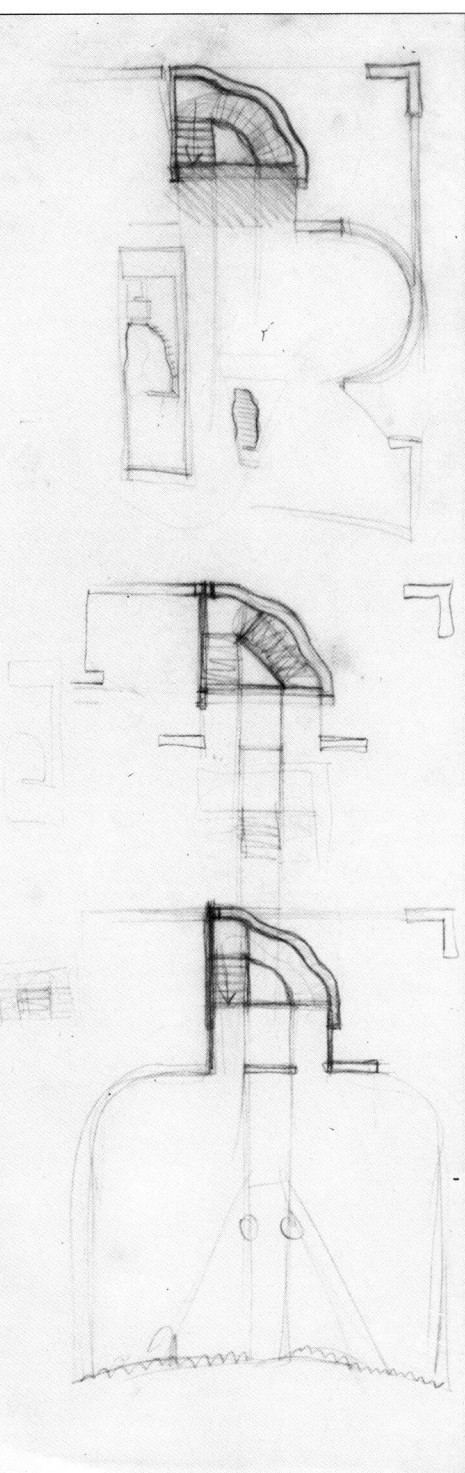

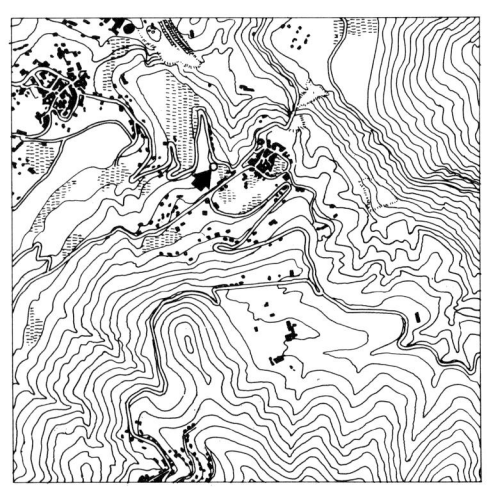

working drawing lower level

Buildings

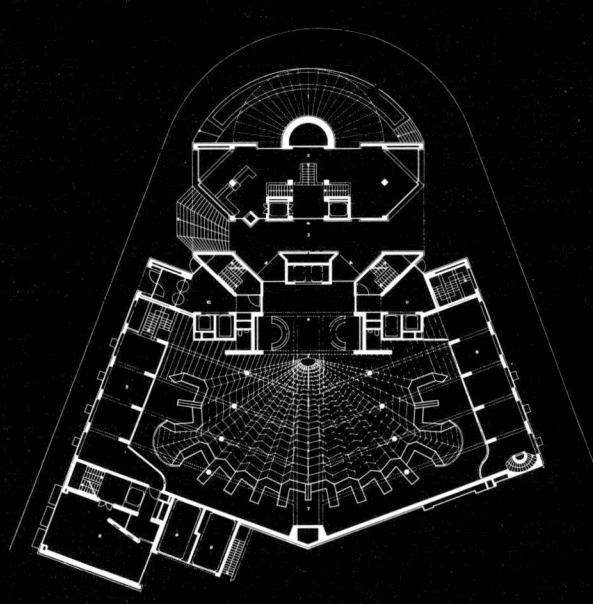

1970   Competition for a school in Locarno, Switzerland

The land lies on the outskirts of Locarno. The school is laid out as a "primary structure," a "finished form" to counter the untidy building all around it.
The project is articulated in three building volumes: the school, the caretaker's lodge and the gymnasium, which intertwine in an area of contact and relationship with the built fabric of the city.
On the three levels the school is set out according to degrees of privacy, whereby the common areas are on the ground floor, the teaching rooms on the second floor and the class-rooms on the third.

The interior space of the different blocks, controlled and articulated autonomously, contrasts with the external space which is treated as a "drawn" element and not as a residual space.

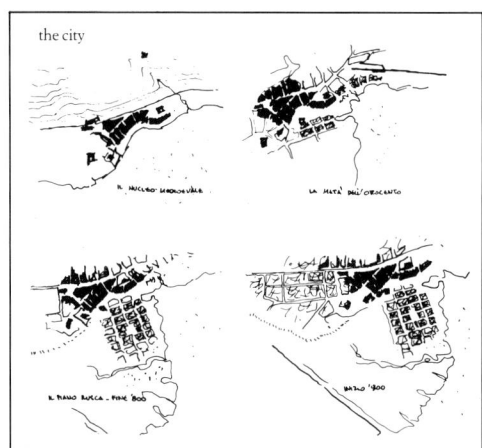

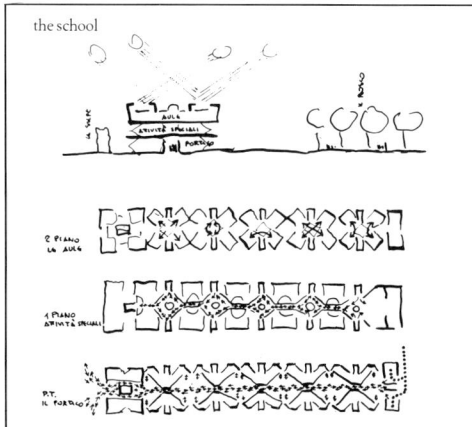

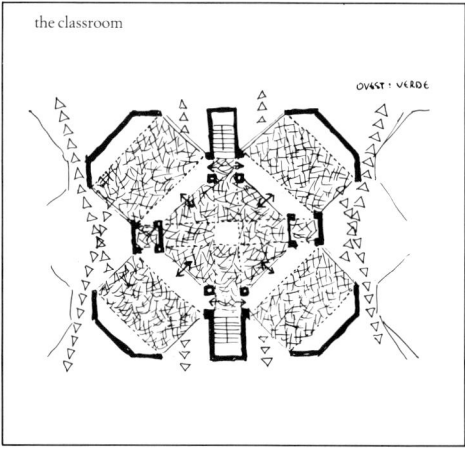

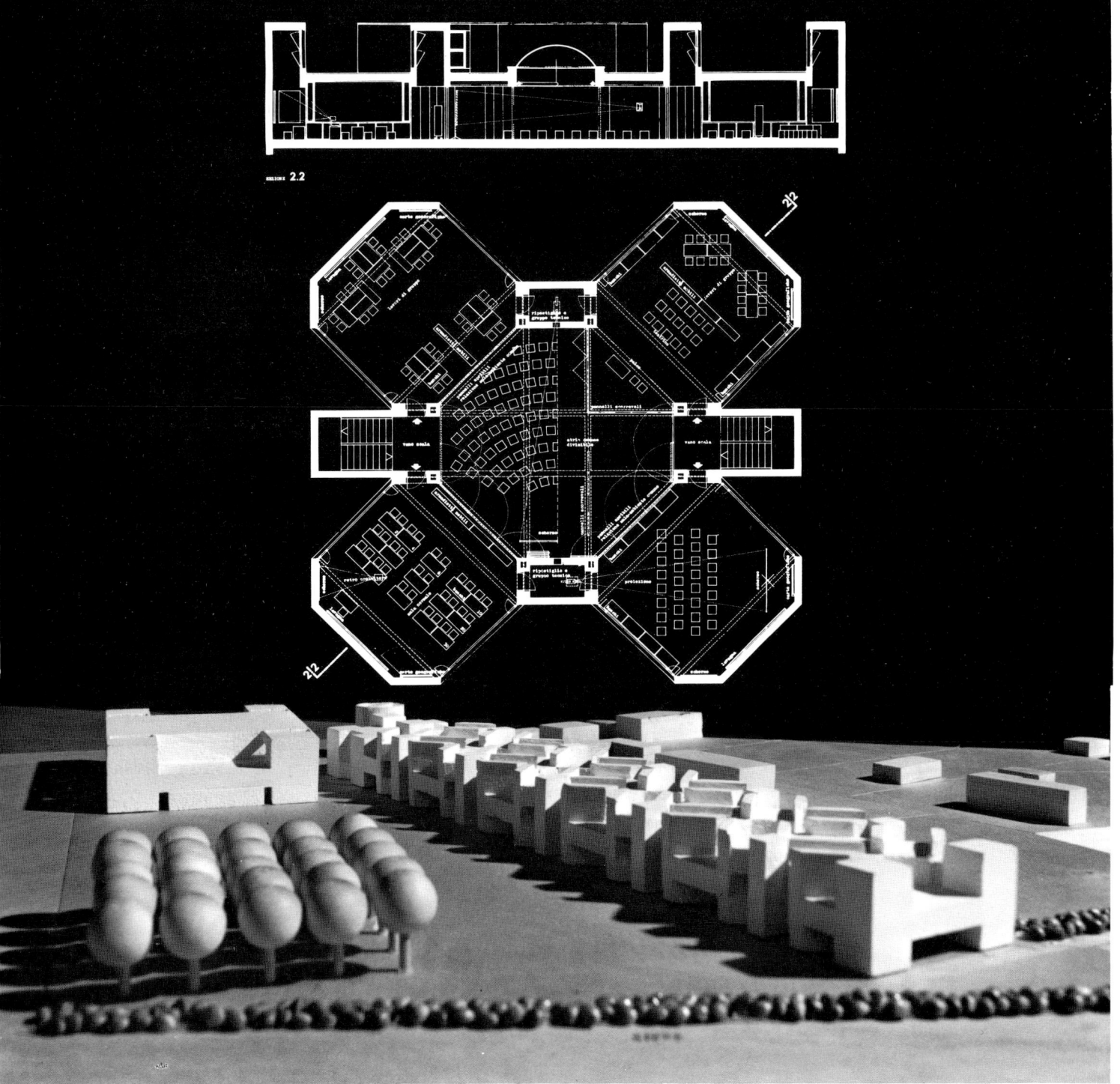

1972-1977   Secondary school in Morbio Inferiore, Switzerland

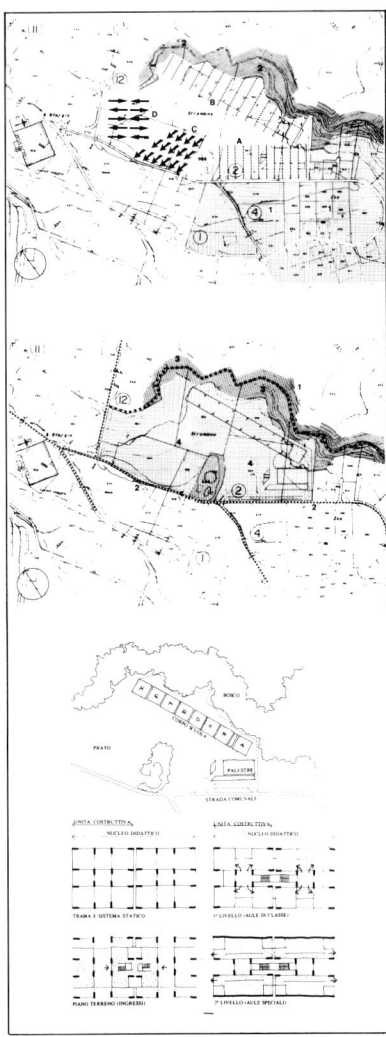

... An isolated architectural project cannot of course alone bring about transformations of sufficient magnitude to concern a whole area. Nevertheless the design can at least take two basic attitudes into account: either to continue to consolidate trends already apparent in the present organization (or disorganization) or attempt to devise alternative proposals with the intent to foster a different structuring of local environmental values so as to strike a new balance between the environment and man's appreciation of it. This second prospect, in which the goals of a project are progressively made clear, brings out the need for a different concept of place which allows an awareness of the characteristic environmental and historical values of a site to be treated as a priority factor in the architect's work today... In other words the aim is to gain, through architecture, an awareness of the cultural values peculiar to a site, as the testimony of a heritage to be regained and brought into the life and organization of today's space. From this view-point architecture is seen as a cognitive and operative tool for the creation of a new environmental balance.
With this pledge architecture is recognized as performing a role which exceeds the direct fulfilment of an immediate social need and progressively represents an opportunity for an appreciation of the limits and scope offered by current development. In respect to its surroundings, the architectural design affords an opportunity not to construct on a *site*, but to construct *that site*, so that the architecture can join the new geographical configuration in a direct link with the qualities of history and of memories peculiar to that place, in token of the aspirations and values of contemporary culture.

Extract from the project report

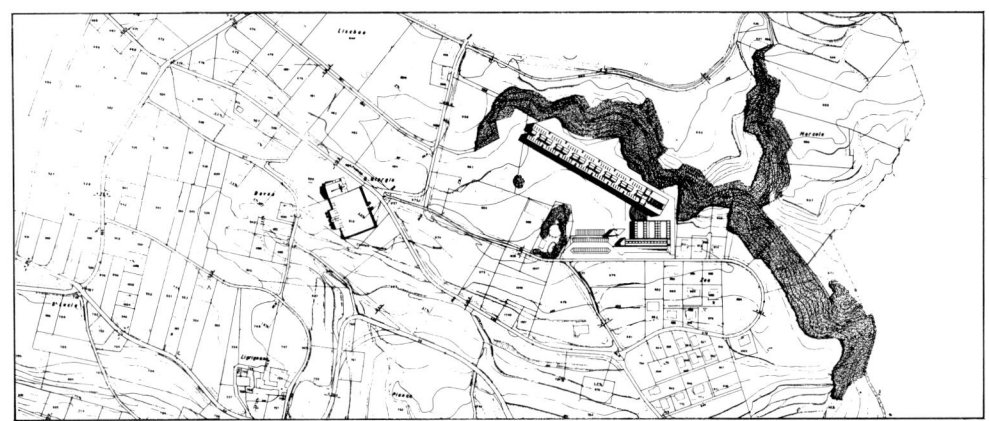

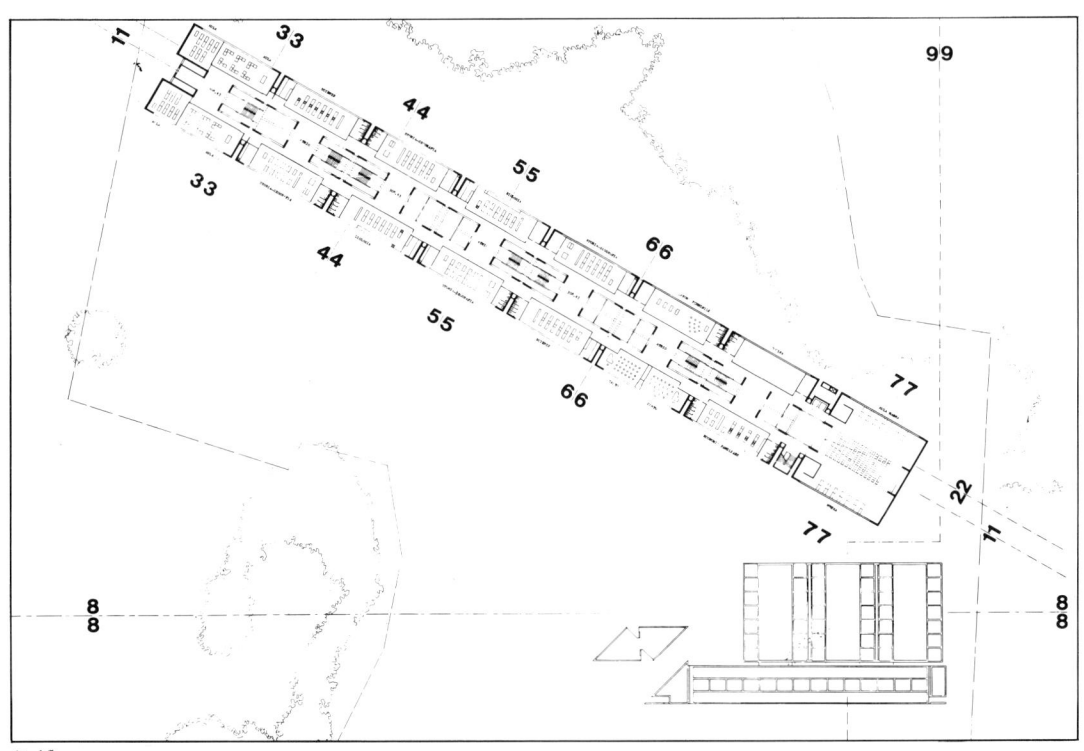

third floor

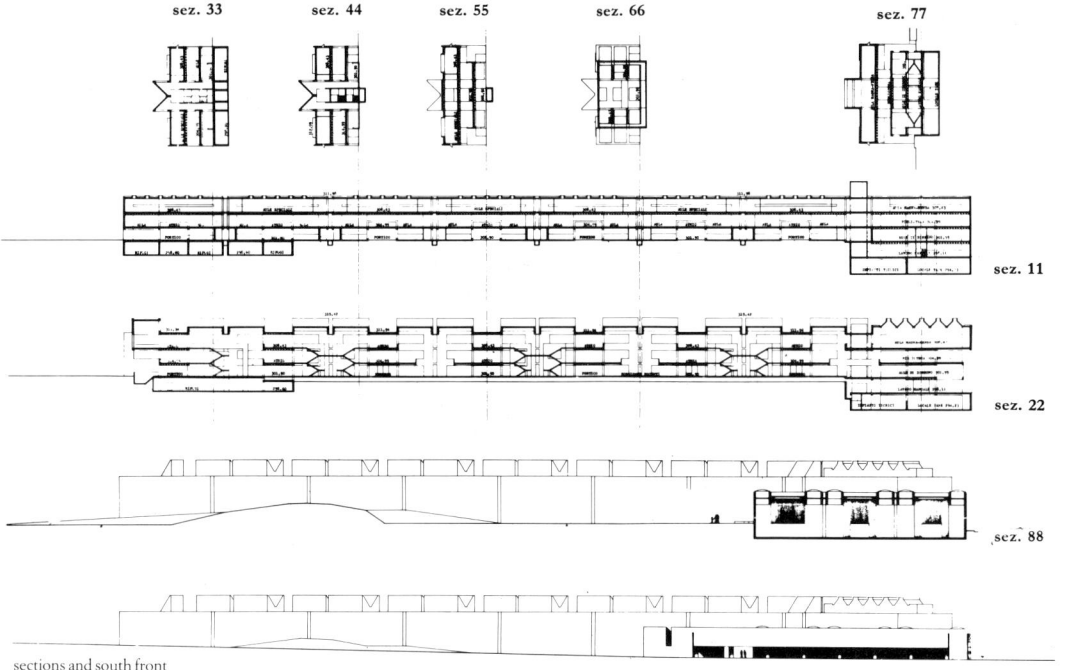

sections and south front

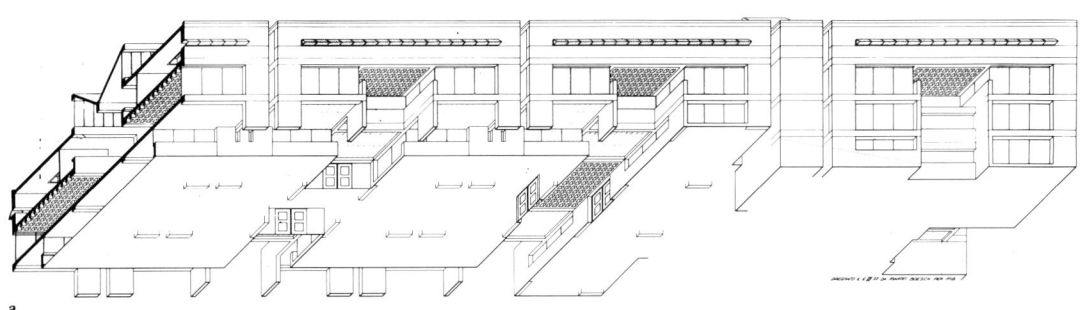

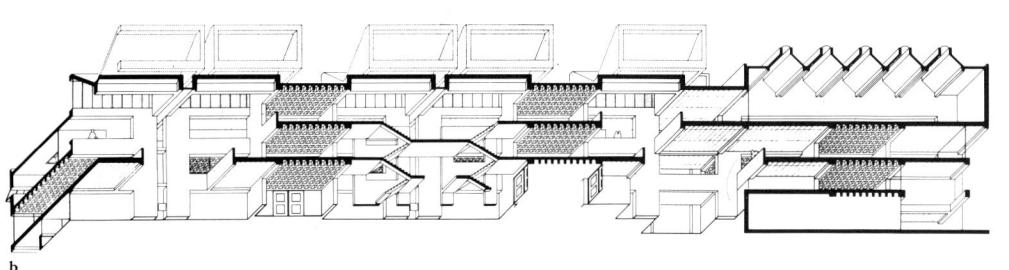

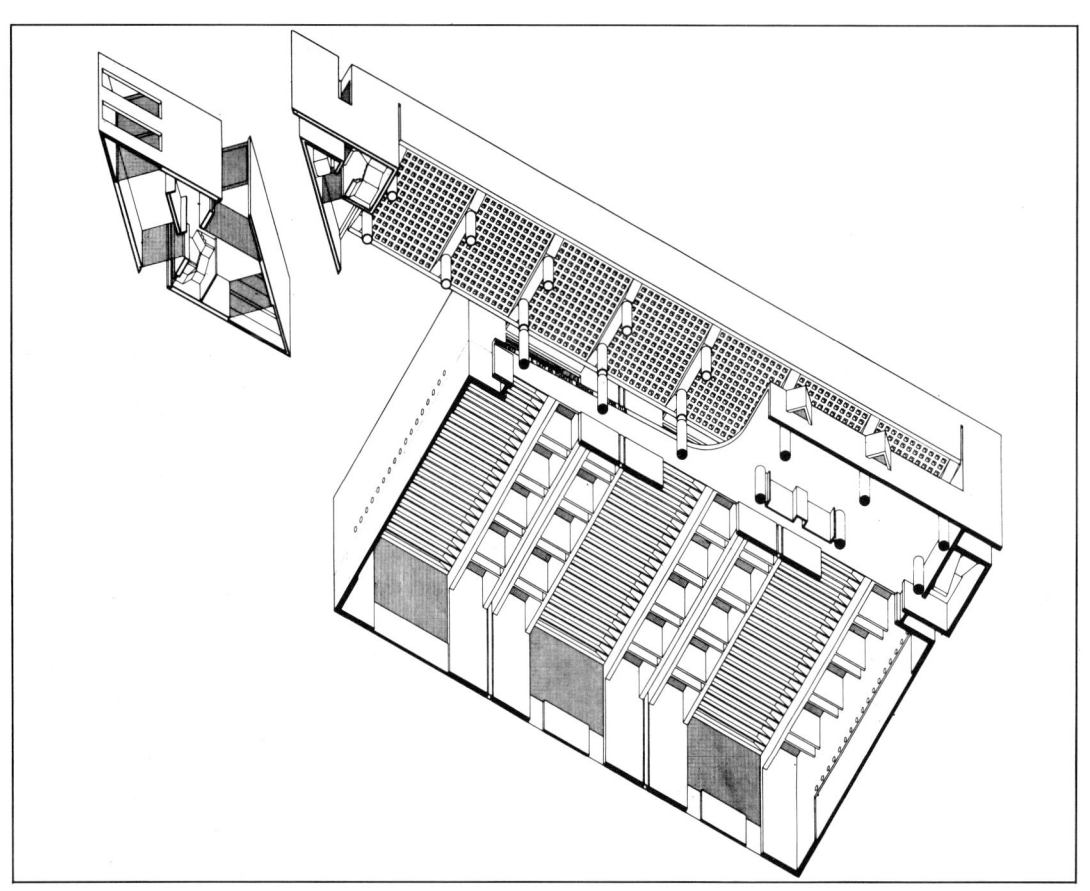

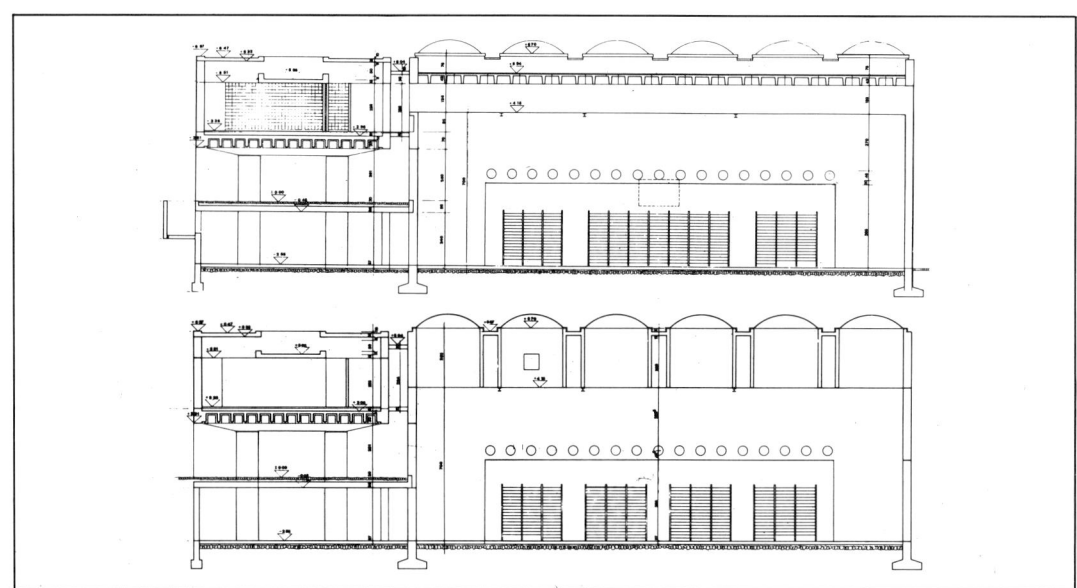

1976-1978   Municipal gymnasium in Balerna, Switzerland

The site chosen by the municipality for this gymnasium (internal space 12 m x 24 m) lies next to the schools in a residential plot. The site has its north front on the access road which runs along the side of the school building. The ground plan was determined by the compulsory setback lines.
The enforced planimetric situation, with its impossibility of lateral building beyond the width of the gymnasium space (12 m) suggested the organization of services (entrance, equipment storage, corrective physical training room, changing rooms, showers, etc.) on the north front of the building.
This part of the building is divided into three different levels and planimetrically shows a division with two building blocks separated asymmetrically from the longitudinal axis of the gymnasium. These building blocks at the top end articulate the entrance space, off which a skylight develops along the whole block and illuminates the interiors from above.
The walls of the building are in light insulating concrete with a transparent pale blue-pink wash on the inside surfaces.
The floors are in prefabricated caisson units to provide good sound insulation. The flooring is in a green synthetic material. Door and window frames are in black thermo-lacquered iron sections. The square in front is paved with porphyry cubes.

1976-1979

Library of the Capuchin monastery in Lugano, Switzerland

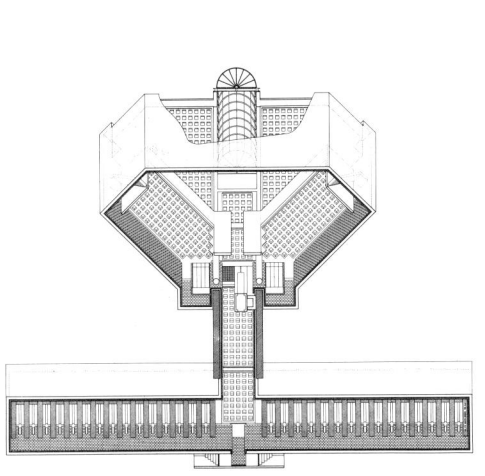

Composed mainly of a reading room and stacks for around 100,000 volumes, this structure is functionally linked to other areas of the adjacent monastery dating from the 17th century.
Built entirely below ground, this new building benefits nevertheless from a generous amount of overhead lighting supplied by a central glass frame (that emerges in the garden as a glasshouse), which permits a direct visual relationship between the reading room and the external configuration of the church and the monastery.

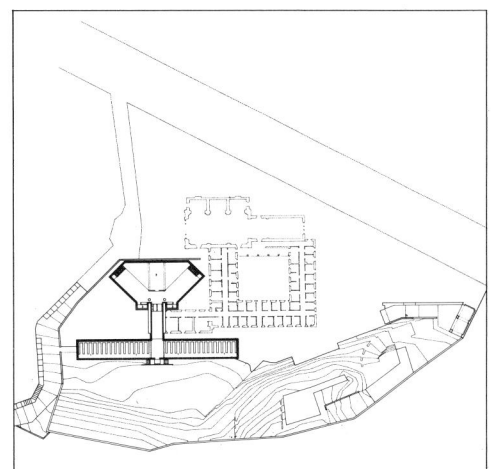

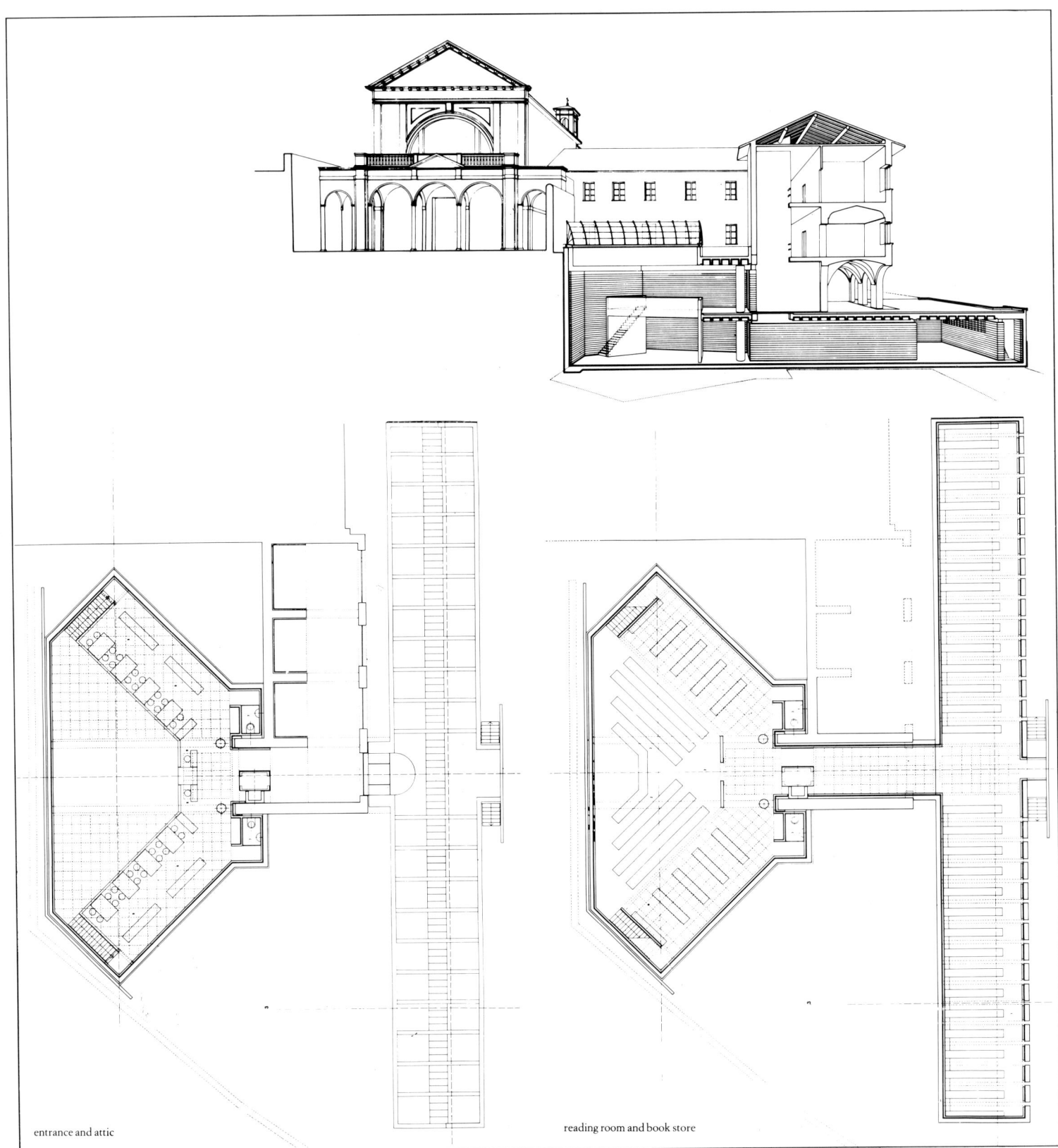

entrance and attic

reading room and book store

1978-1979

Transformation and re-use of a farmhouse in Ligrignano, Chiasso, Switzerland

The farm buildings are on a plateau within the municipal territory of Morbio Inferiore, immediately above the Chiasso plain.
The farm covers the end of a natural promontory whose geographical boundaries are emphasized by a compound of perimeter walls enclosing the different farm areas.
The different functions that were originally performed there are still distinct and organized according to different buildings and spaces, stables and outhouses, yards, vegetable gardens and farm land.
The redevelopment project involved a part of this complex, namely, the land situated on the east front. It is articulated in three structures: the house itself, the courtyard, the barn and stables.
The project set out to underline these three sectors by demolishing and removing the buildings added after the original. The yard (space relating the house to the stables) was rebuilt along the whole of the west front where a new boundary wall has been erected to close the old entrance. The demolition of an old building along this front allowed a new open space (external living room) to be regained. This transformed what was an indoor space (with fireplace and window) into an outdoor one. In this way the functional (interior as a defensive space) and the spatial (the window as a source of light) relations of the original structure were reversed.

before restoration

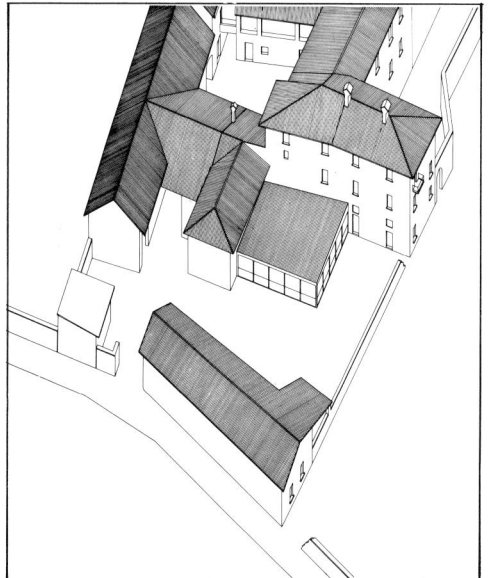

after restoration

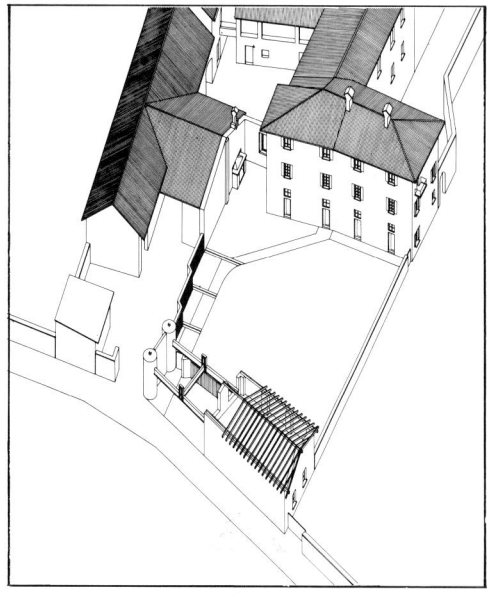

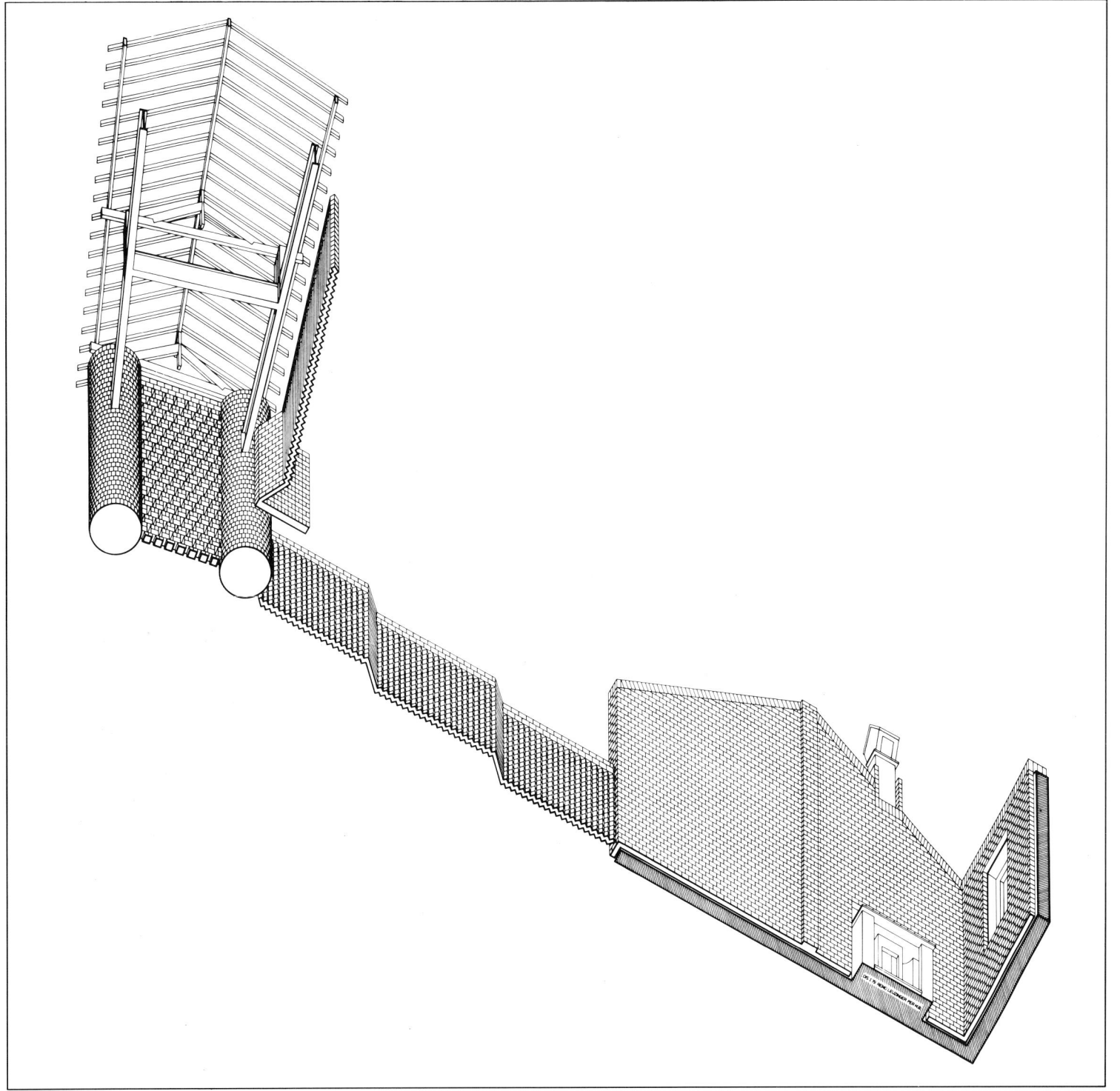

1977-1979　　　　　　　　**Artisan center in Balerna, Switzerland**

A structure with four buildings for artisan activities: each comprising a workshop on the ground floor, offices on the second and living on the third. It is set in a suburb of Chiasso characterized by "spontaneous" urbanization with all the entailing disorder.
The four buildings organized around a courtyard covered by a glazed metal frame stand as elements of order, a formal reference point in the chaotic surrounding agglomeration.

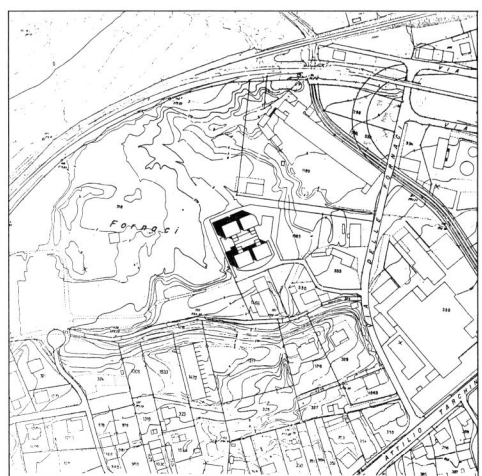

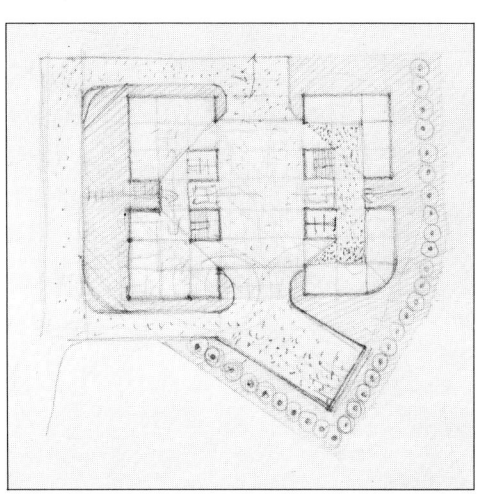

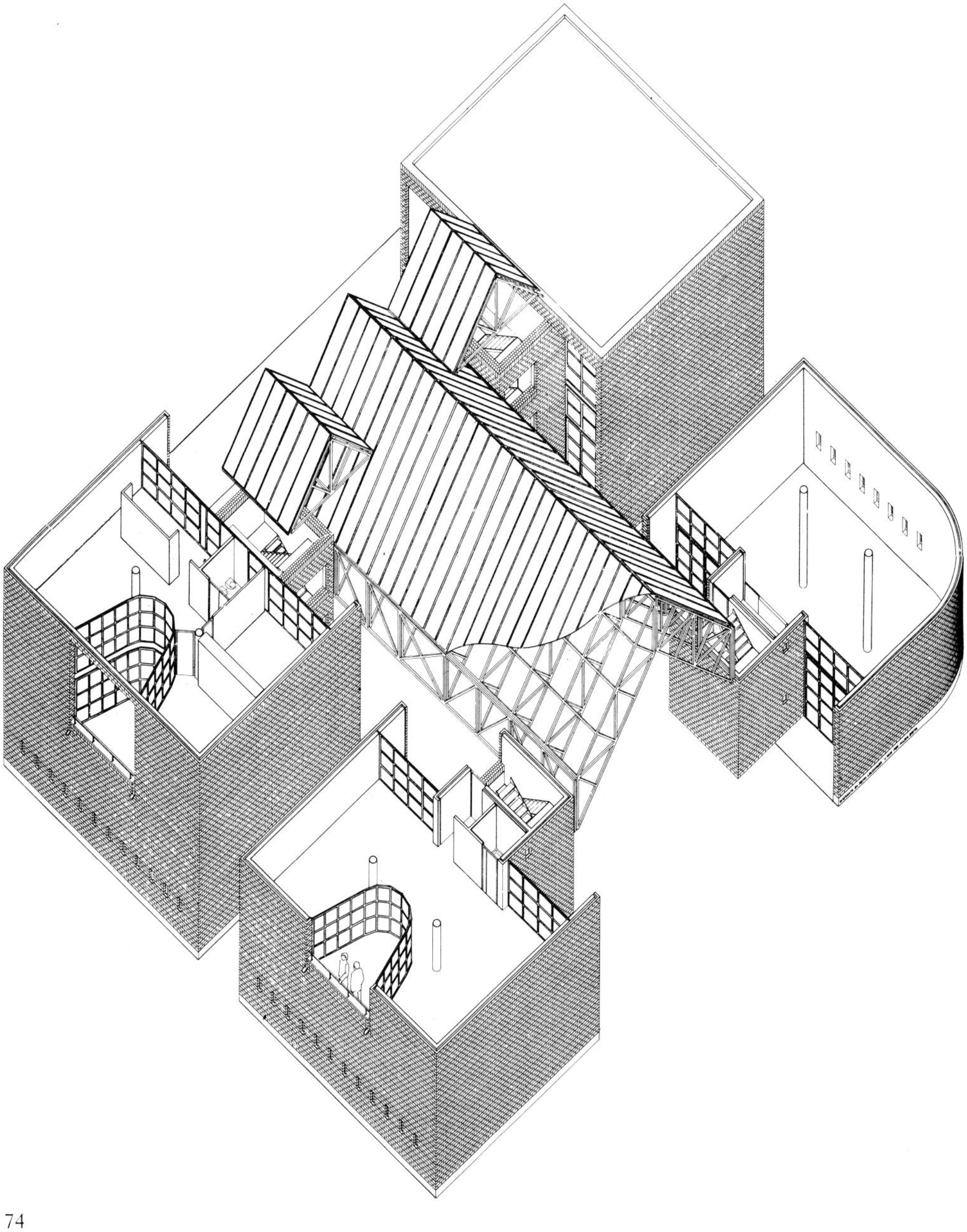

1977-1982   **State Bank in Freiburg, Switzerland**

The triangular-shaped site chosen for the BEF seems particularly well-suited and suggestive. In the project, the position at the corner of an urban lot brings out the different typological characteristics of this singular location.
The building is divided into three volumes (two lateral wings and a central building) which present different architectural expressions. The two wings form elements of continuity with the urban fabric of the last century. The main building contrasts more freely with the open space of the square.
The way in which the walls and the openings of the new building are handled emphasize, in the lateral sections, a characteristic element of the boulevard. The central part underlines the alteration and articulation with an architectural language of the urban fabric at this location and responds in a similar manner to the different conditions of the street on the sides and that of the square in the central section.
Its location at the heart of the urban fabric makes the building a new reference point for the whole of the station square.

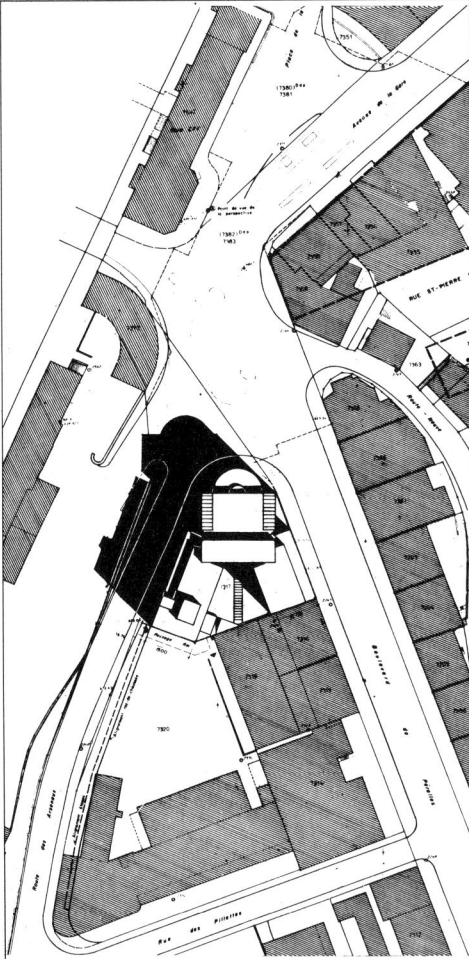

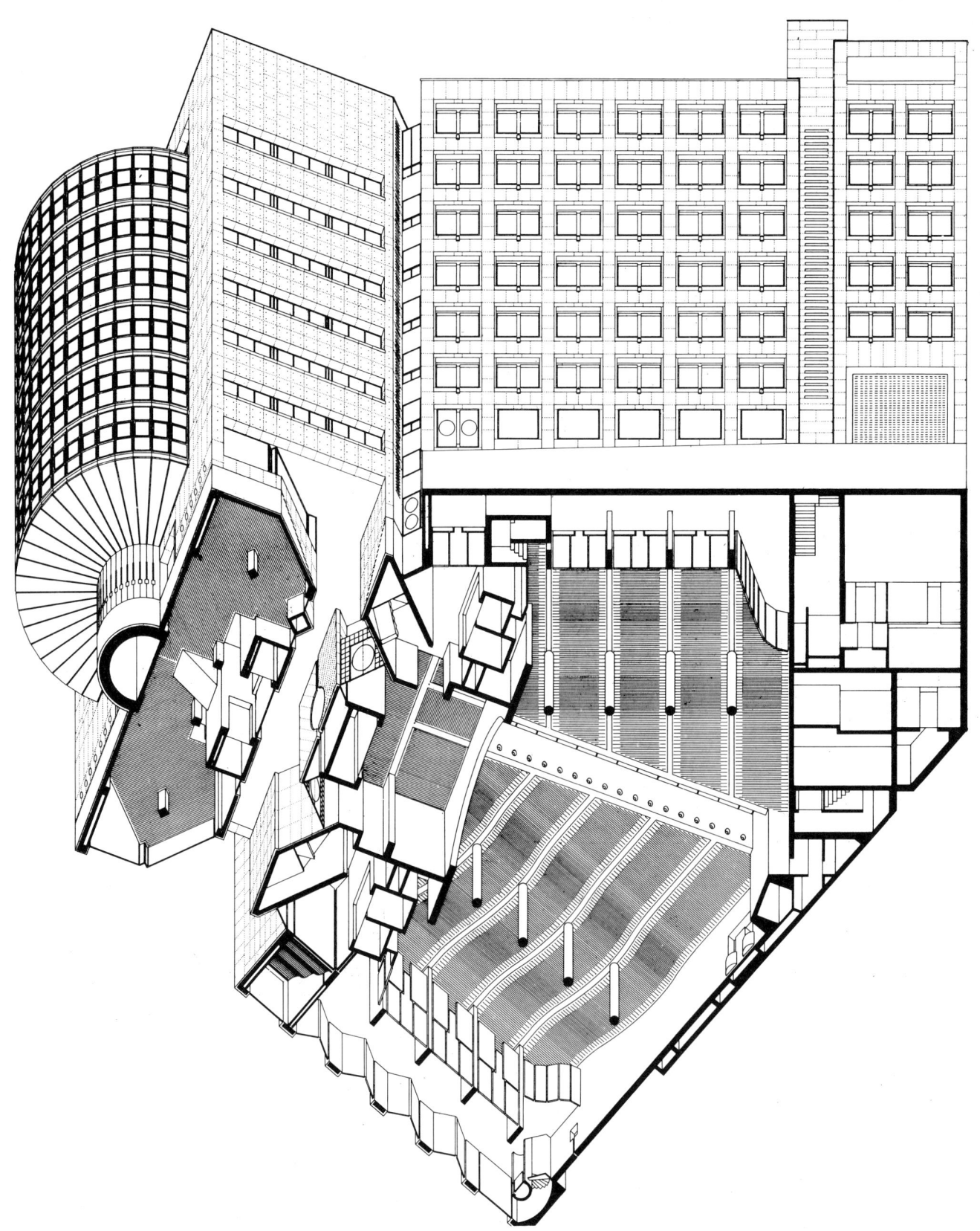

1979

Project for an artisan building in Balerna, Switzerland

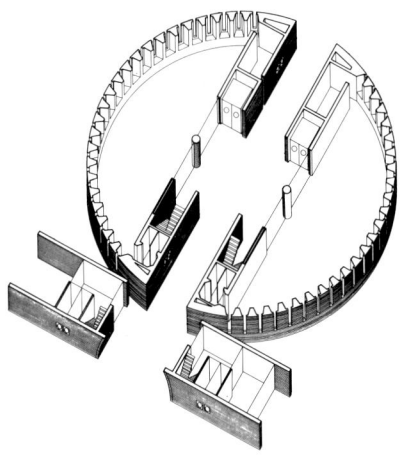

The triangular site is residual land bordered by the railway line, a stream and on the south side by the access route. The scheme called for two areas to be assigned as workshops-cum-stores as well as two apartments for artisan or caretakers. The project provided two buildings for the different functions separated from each other by a vertical central path.
On the side of the road, the south-facing residences form the access building to the workshop-storehouse in the rear which is a large cylindrical building.

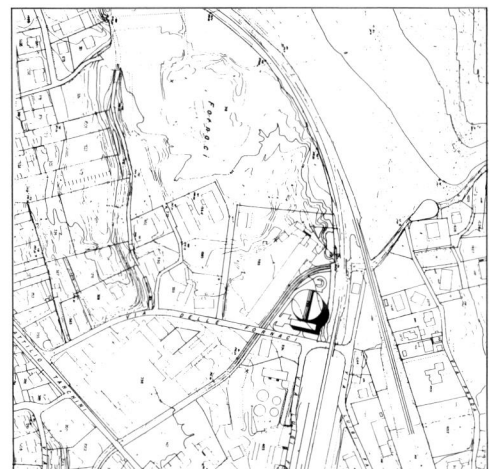

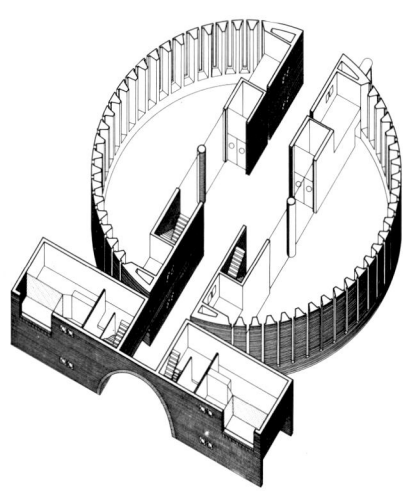

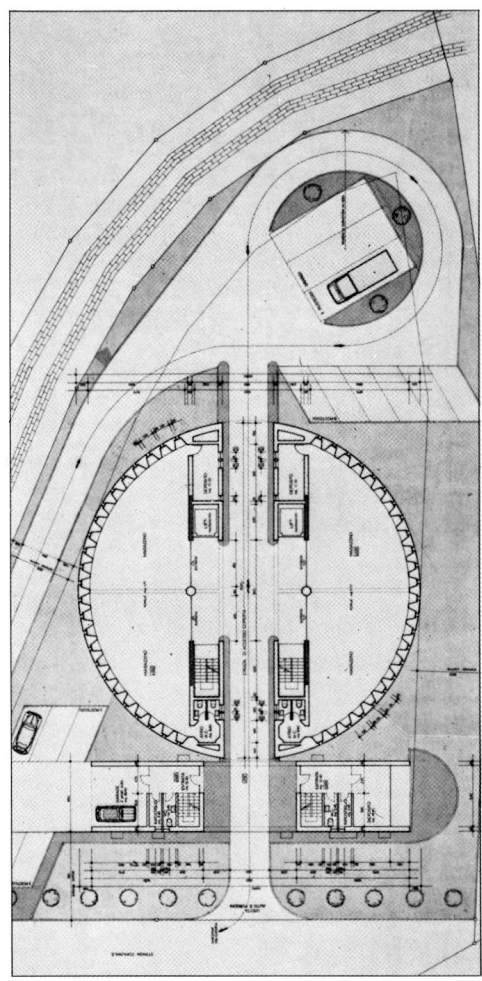

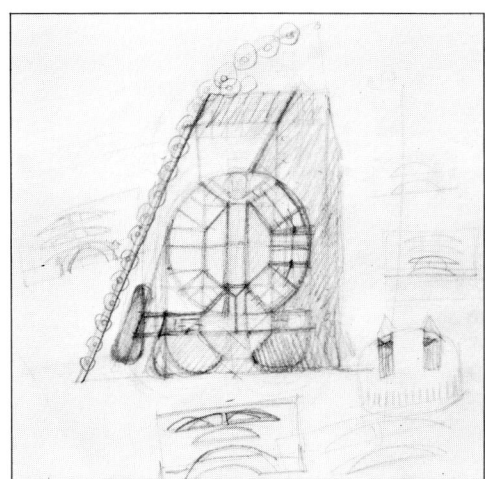

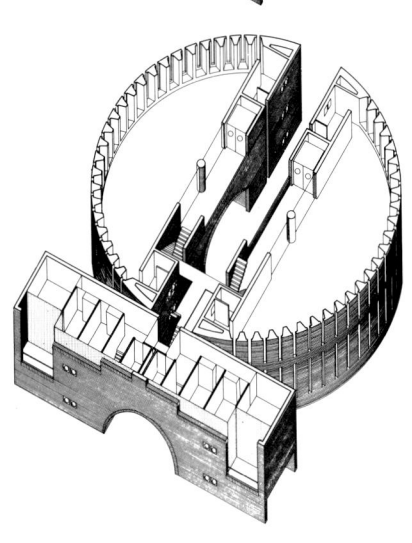

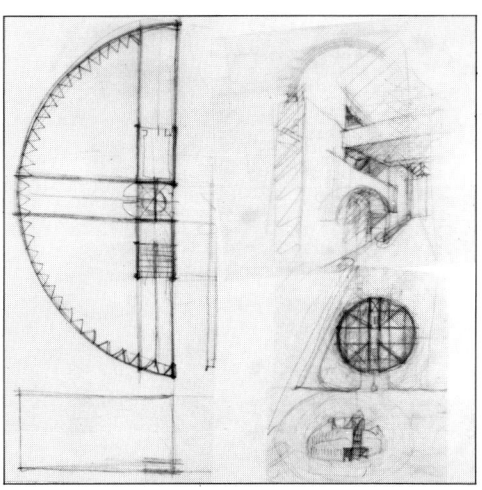

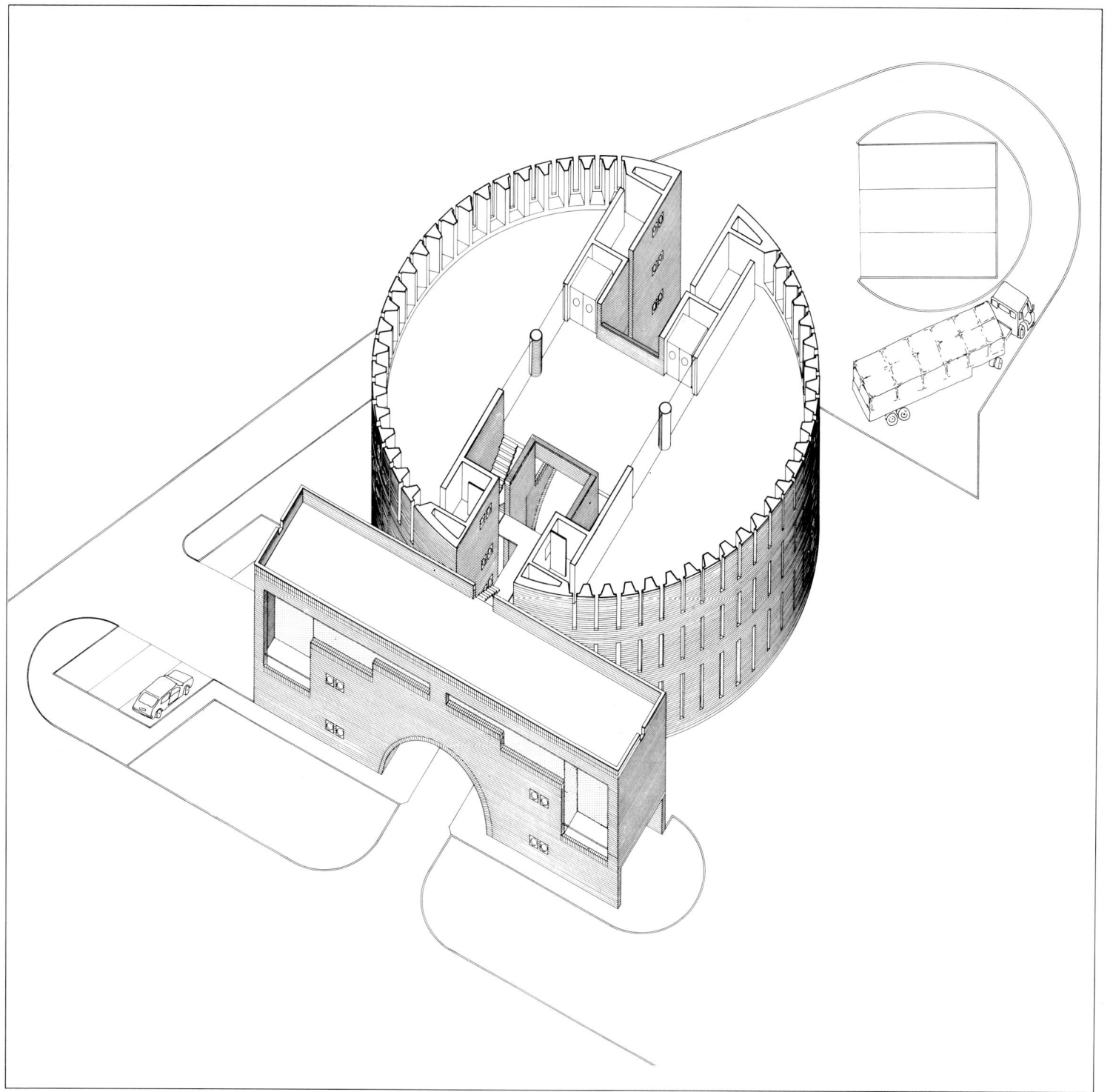

1980

Competition for an administrative and reception building in Brühl, West Germany

The competition held for DOM called for an administrative building to be erected alongside the existing factory. Its main function was to exert a strong appeal for publicity purposes.
The proposed building stands in the landscape like a screen held at its extremities by the vertical circulation towers.
The two main facades would be faced with glass blocks and an aperture in the form of a portal transverses the building in an extension of the entrance way.

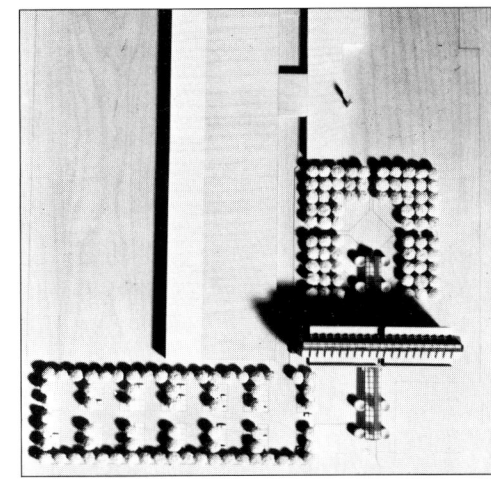

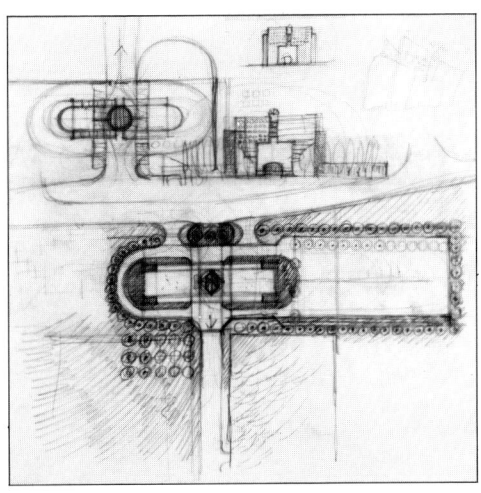

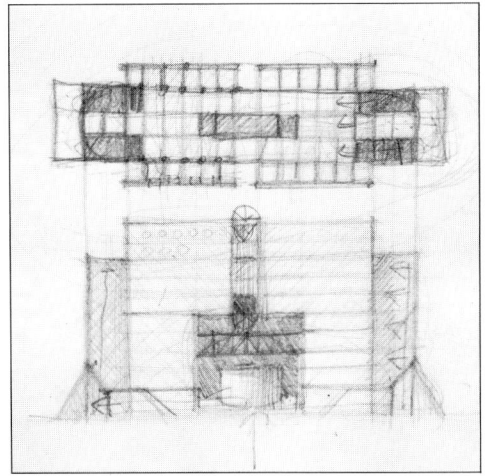

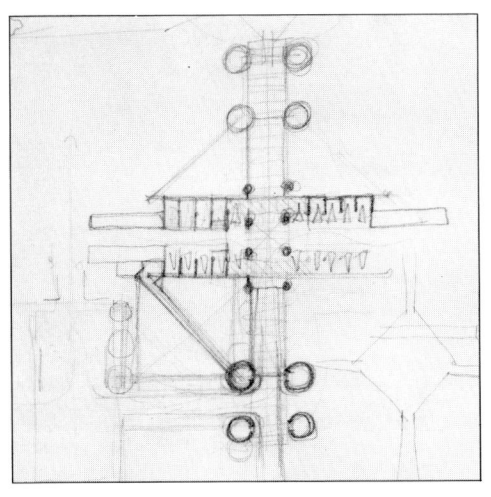

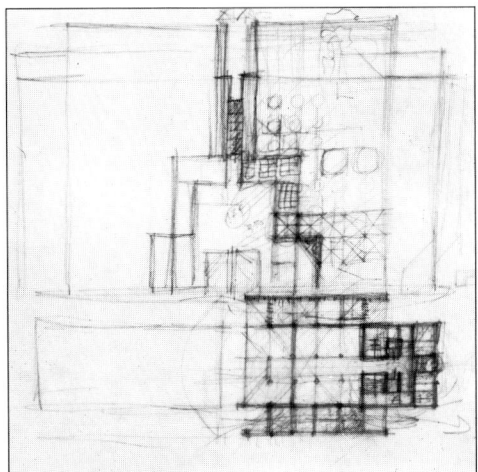

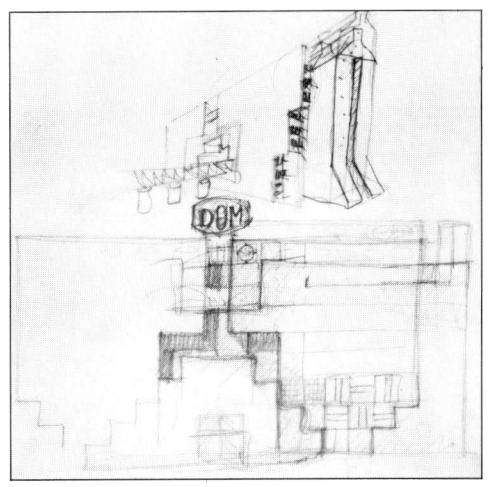

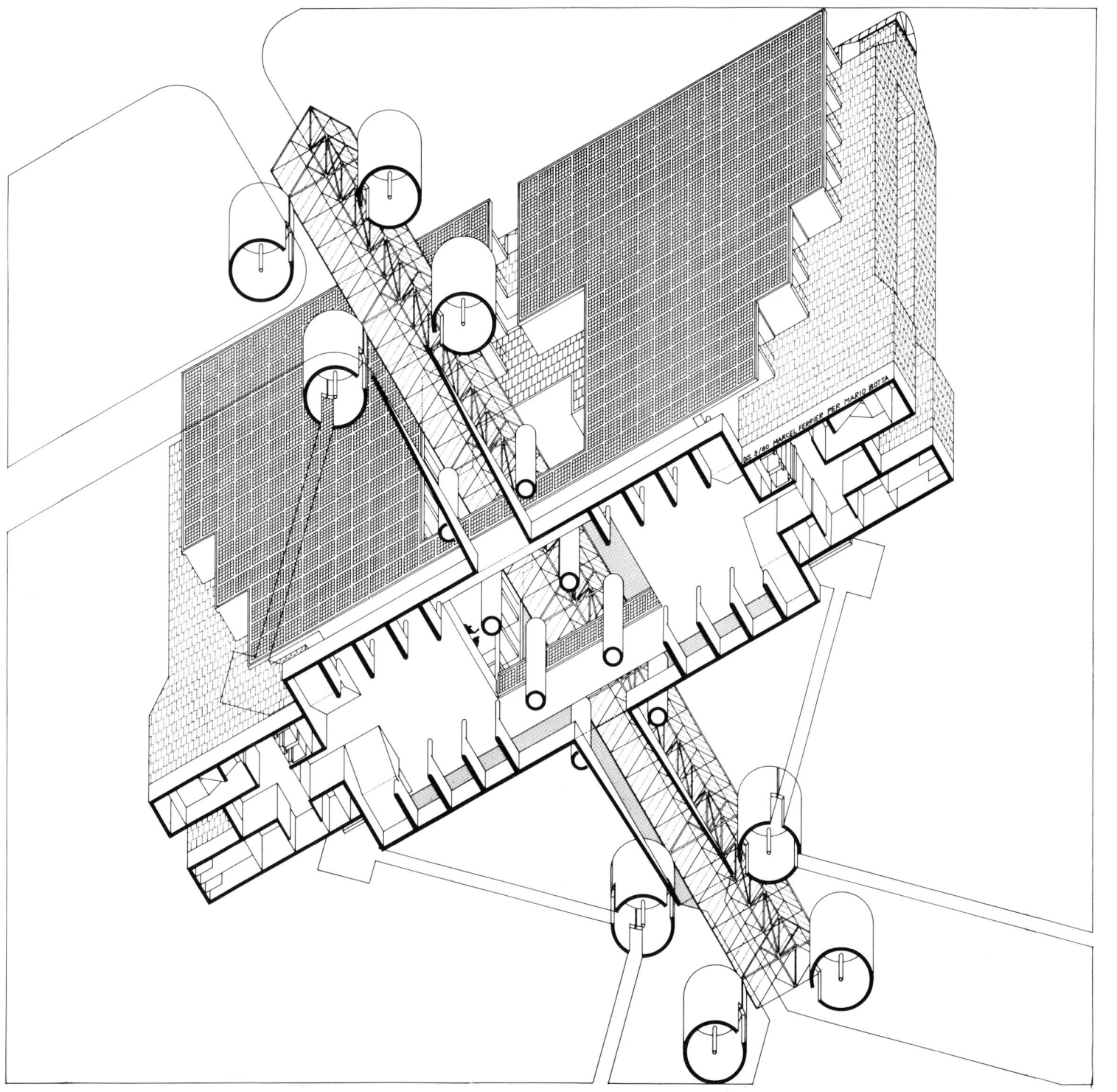

1980   Project for a clinic in Agra, Switzerland

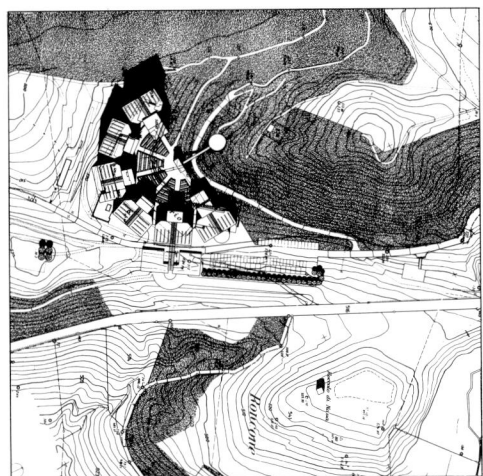

Because of the site's location on sunlit slopes and looking out over a magnificent landscape, the six towers have been arranged in a fan shape, the residential parts of which are towards the exterior on an 180° angle. The central space brings together all the functions of access, distribution and living formulated in the program.
The aim of the project is to define a huddled, compact grouping, a kind of community capable of relating and contrasting with the surrounding scenery.

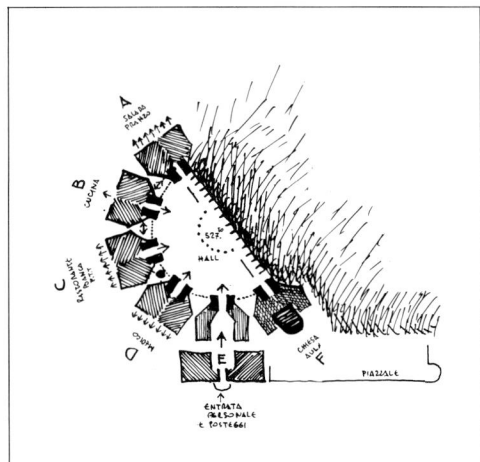

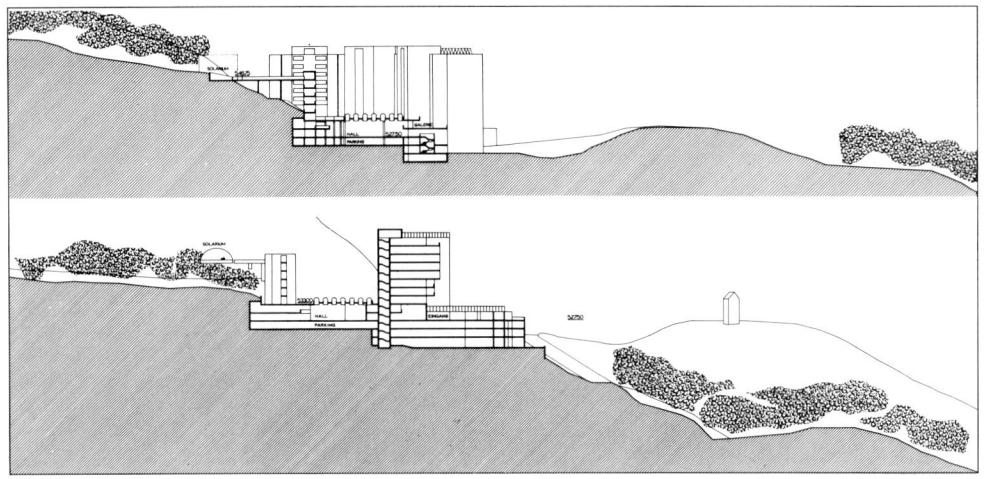

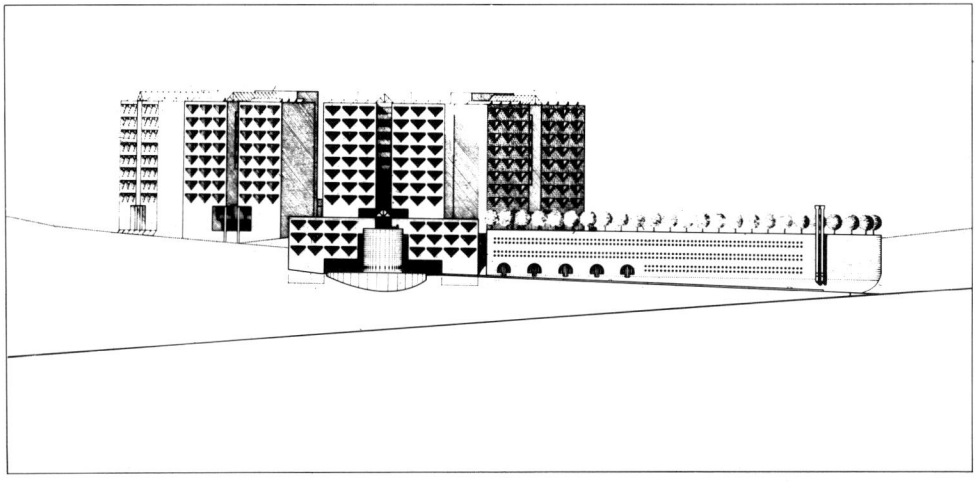

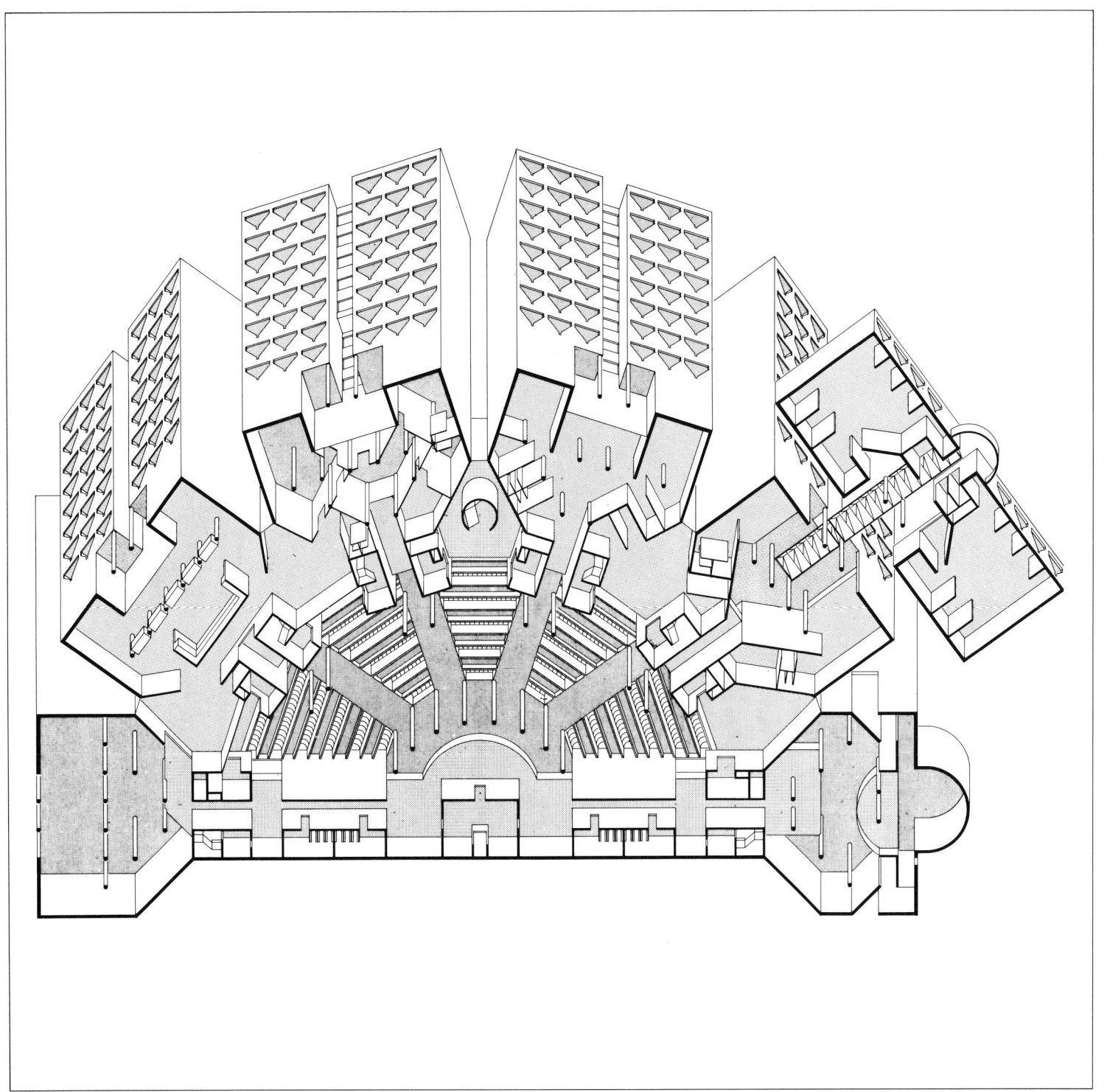

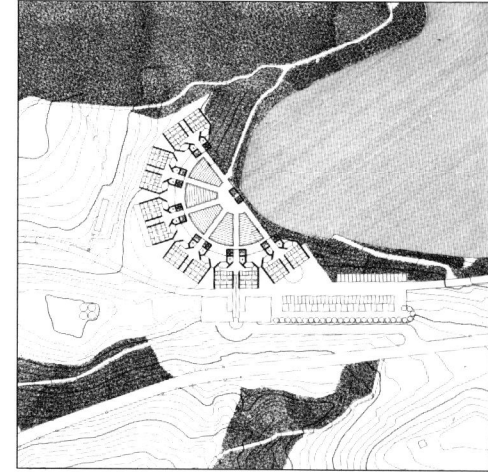
standard floor

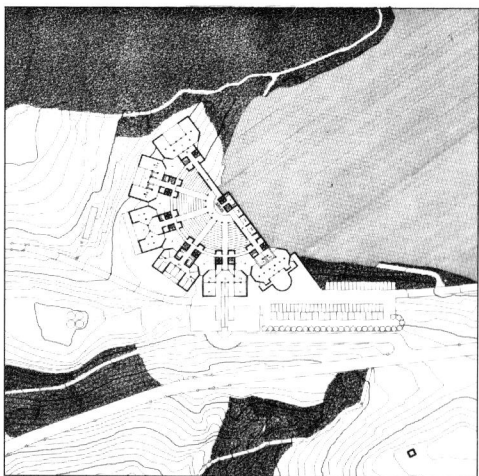
basement

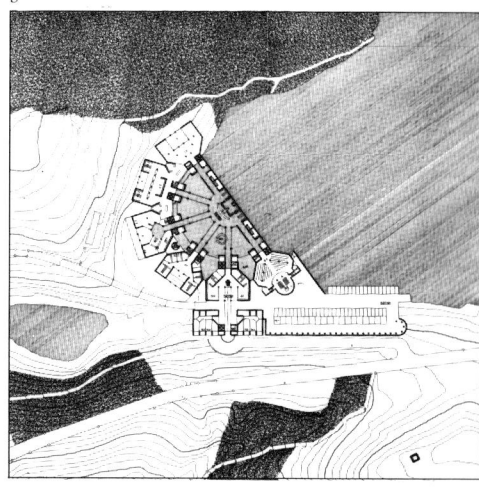
ground floor

1981 — Project for the Guernica Museum in Guernica, Spain

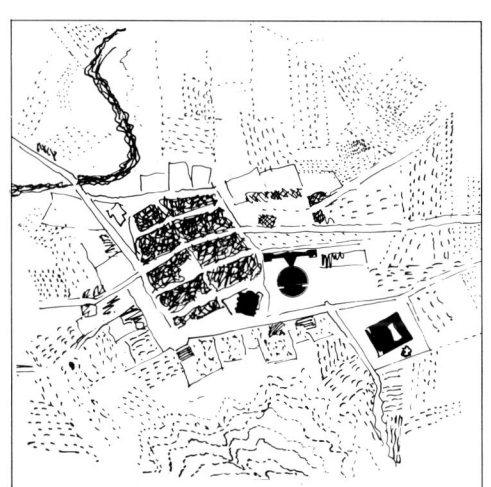

"Designing a space for *Guernica* is an act of joy, a moment of faith, an occasion for prayer."
The project proposes a central sunken space between the two neoclassical existing school buildings. The circular space ends at the rear wall where the *Guernica* painting is hung, surrounded at the perimeter by the preparatory sketches and studies.
The space has a sole source of light that focuses on the picture from above. The intention is to create a space of meditation, of reflection, of well-being and of silence.
A white space.

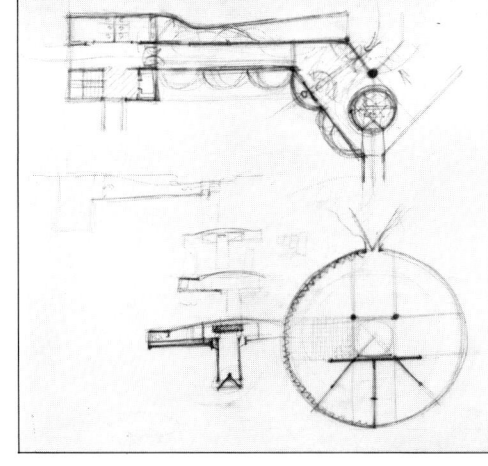

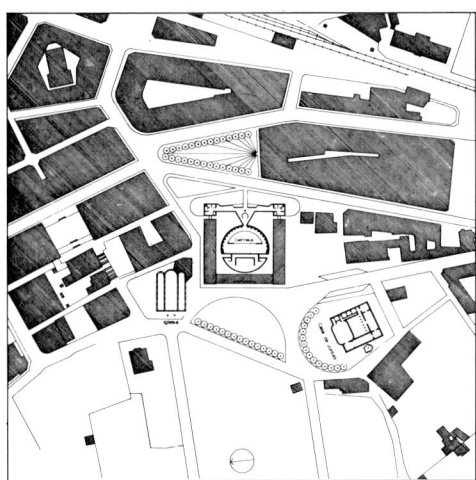

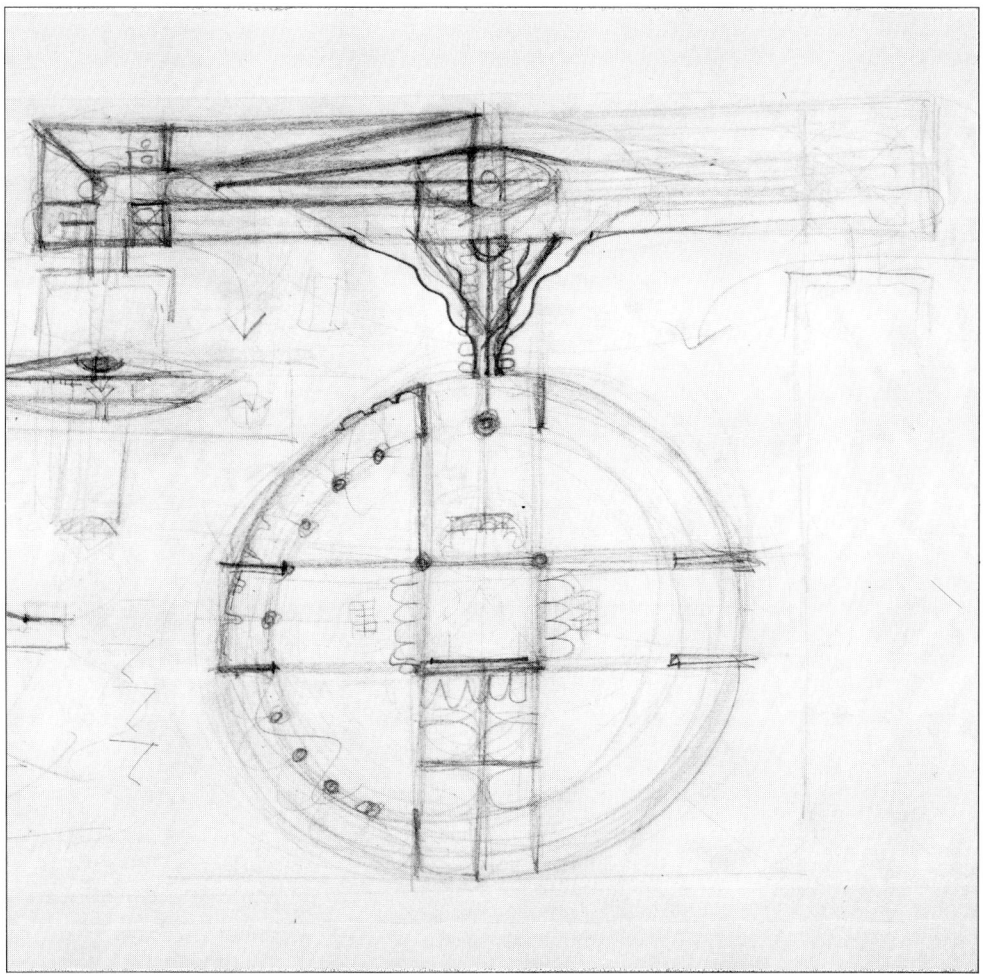

underground museum level

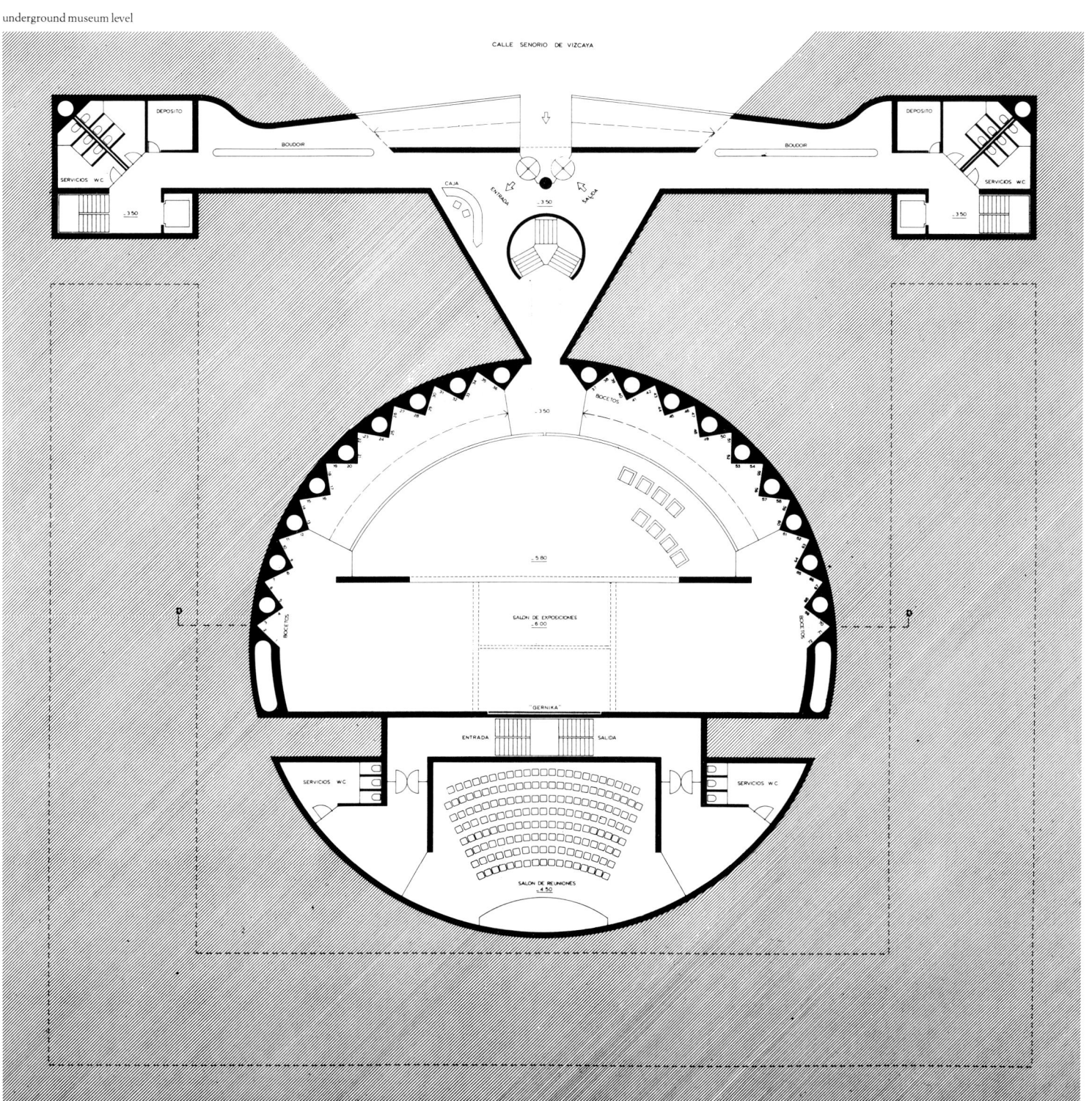

1981 **Administrative and commercial building in Lugano, Switzerland**
(under construction)

The building underlines the theme of the urban corner. The site is open to a square and is on a block of early twentieth century buildings. Through apertures hollowed out of the volume, the project emphasizes a tower that becomes the "hinge" between the two orthogonal facades. A beam-wall delineates the cornice with a pattern of windows in relief, the aim being to accentuate the effect of cavities characteristic of the handling of openings in street frontages.

working drawing second level

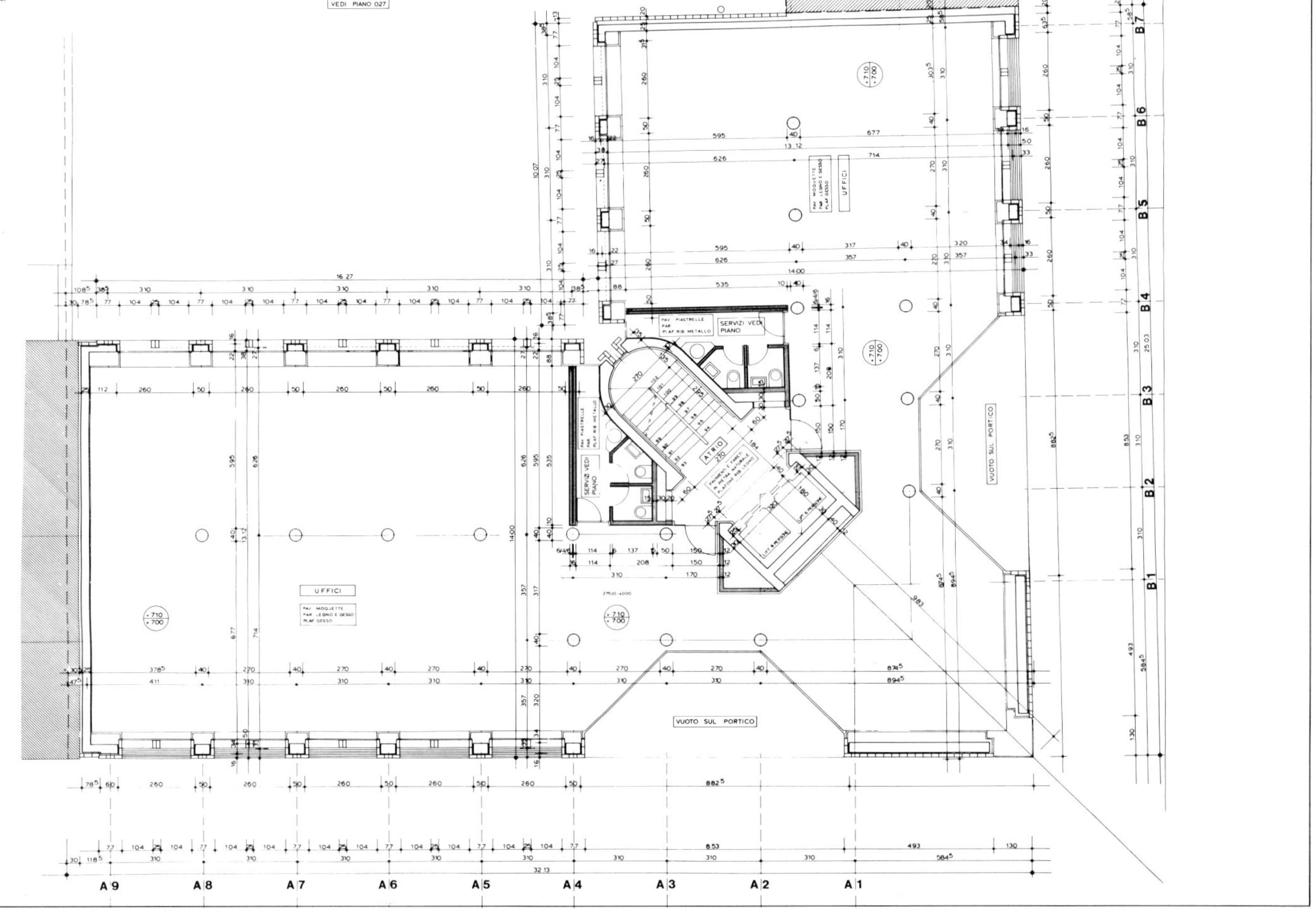

1982　**Maison de la Culture in Chambéry, France**

The project was entered for a competition for a Maison de la Culture as part of the conversion of a wing in the Napoleonic "Curial Barracks." The solution presented the reconstruction of the east wing and the development of a new playhouse to hold around 1000 people.
The project proposes three distinct areas: the adaptation of the east wing for reception facilities, the new rooms situated in a cylindrical volume and the stage structures in the parallelepiped set at the rear.

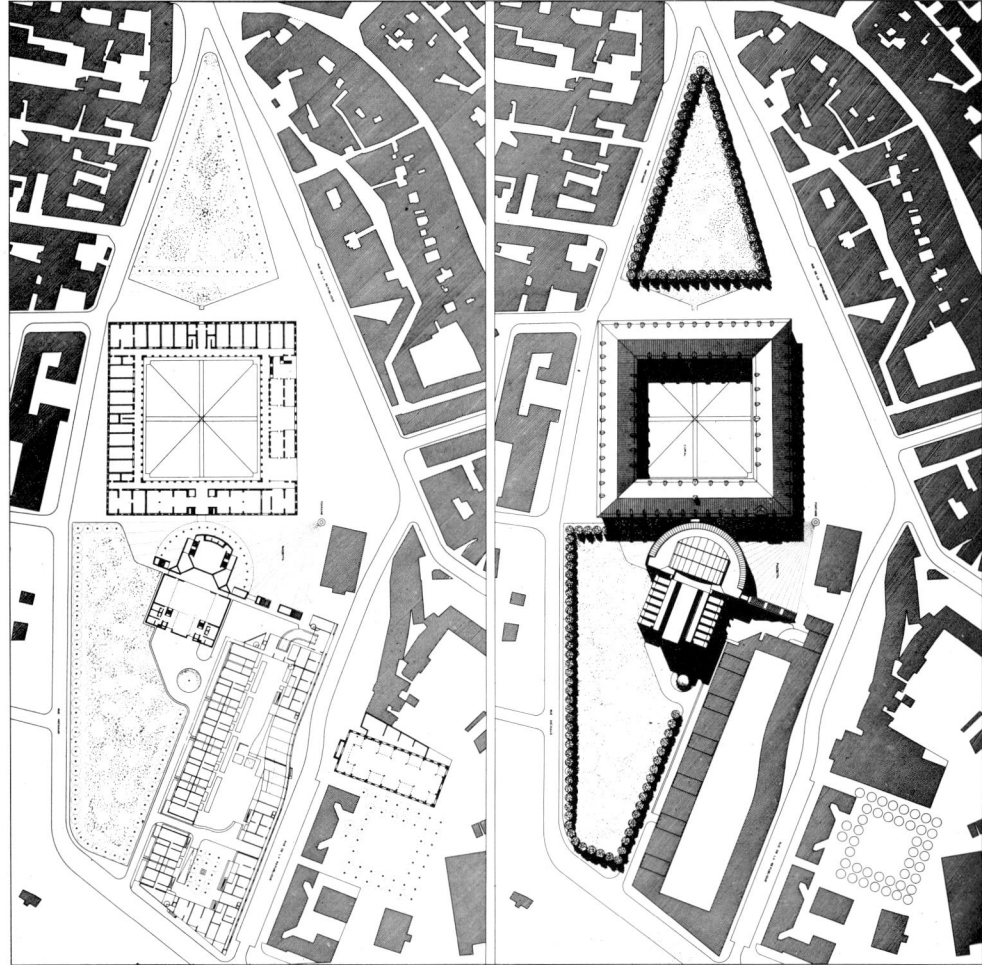

competition project

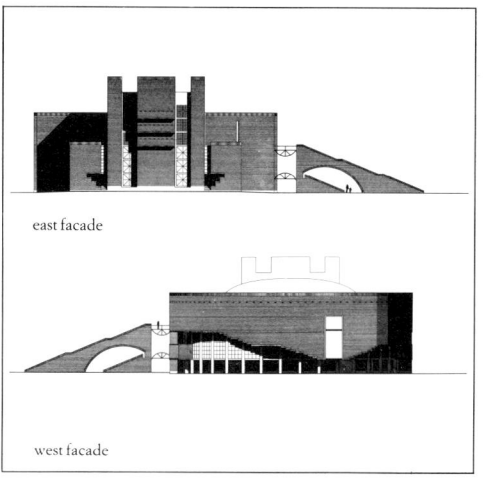

east facade

west facade

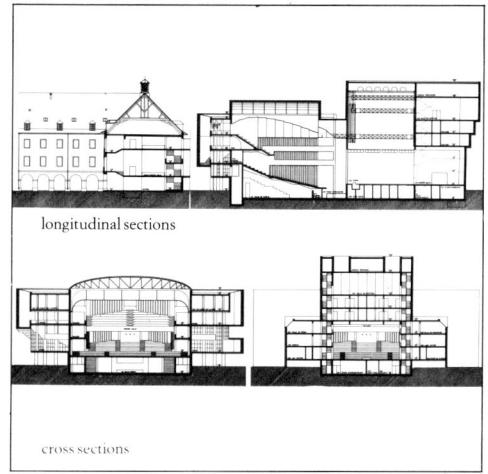

longitudinal sections

cross sections

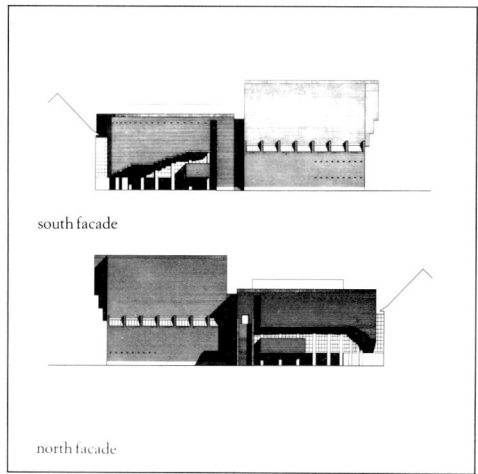

south facade

north facade

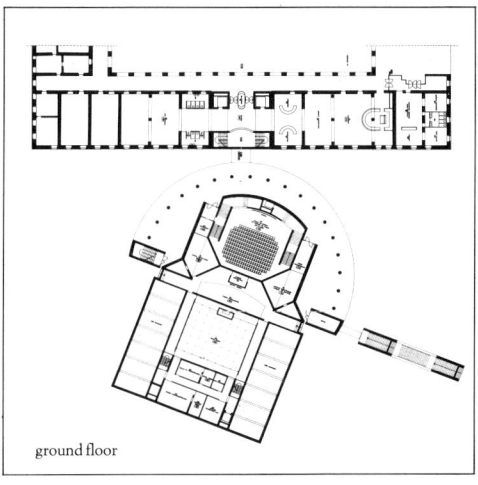

ground floor

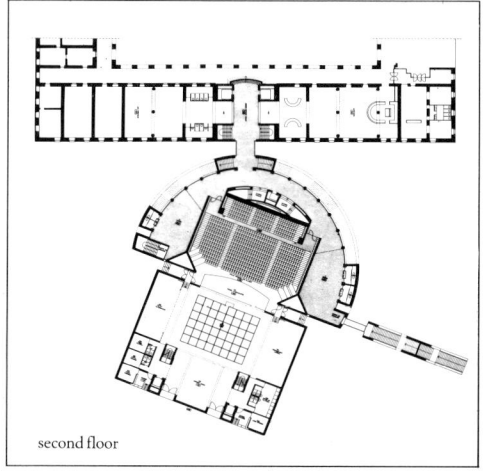

second floor

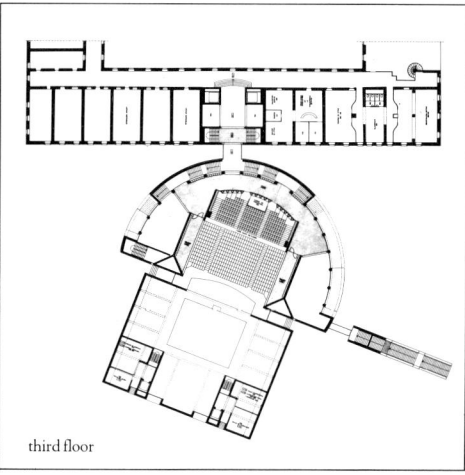

third floor

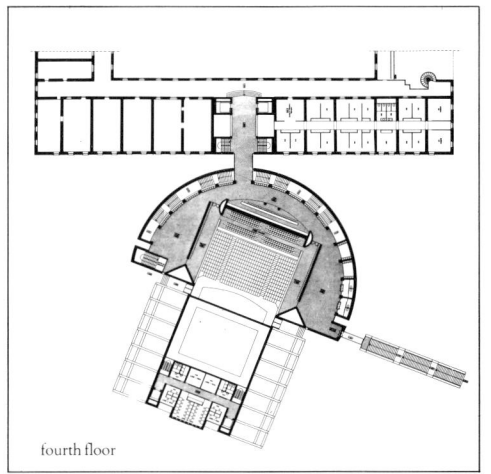

fourth floor

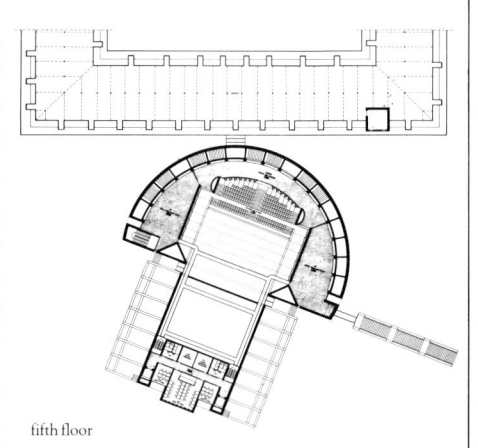

fifth floor

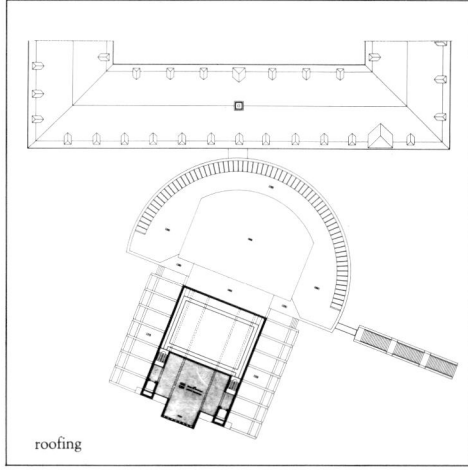

roofing

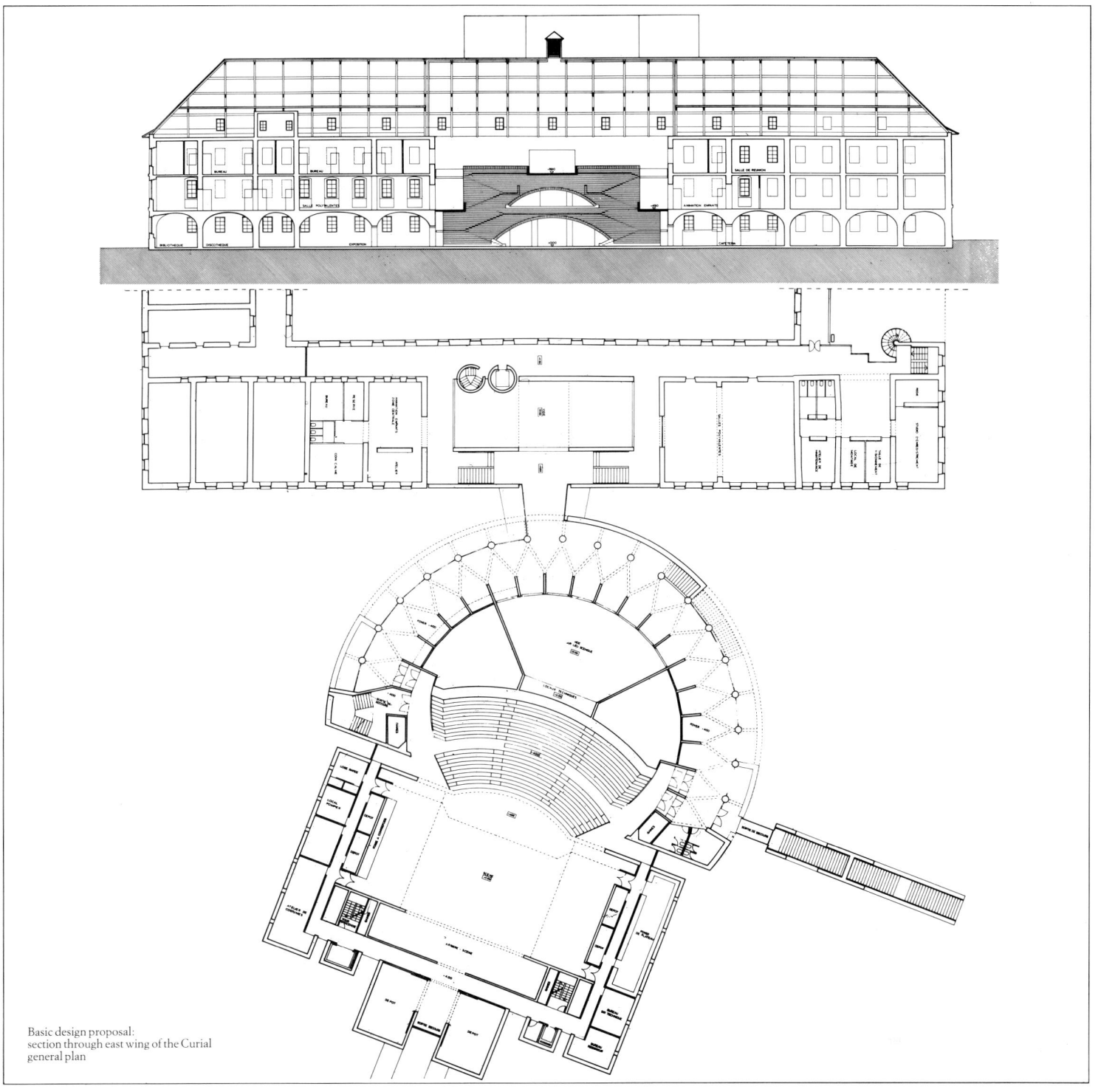

Basic design proposal:
section through east wing of the Curial
general plan

1982   **Project for a building on the square of the TGV station in Lyons, France**

The project proposes a building-cum-gateway which completes the work carried out for the new station square. The building is a symbol of the link between the expanding town and the new high speed train railway station.
The building acts as intermediary between the station traffic and the raised pedestrian foot bridges.

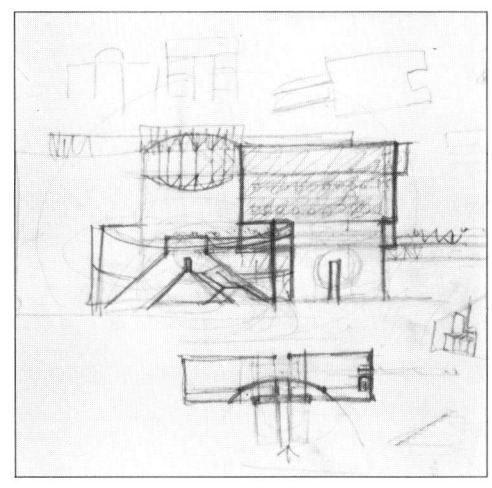

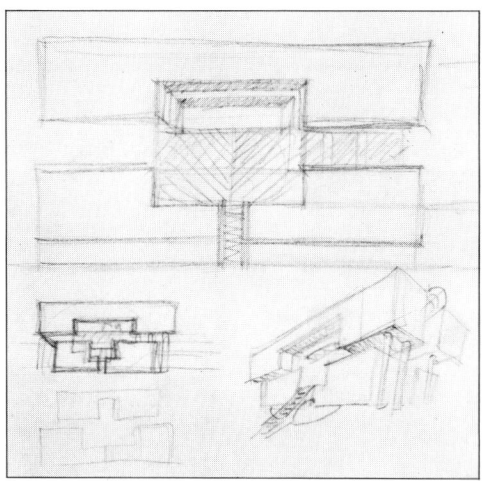

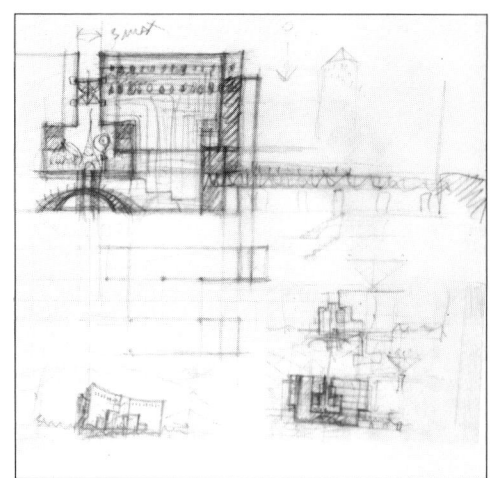

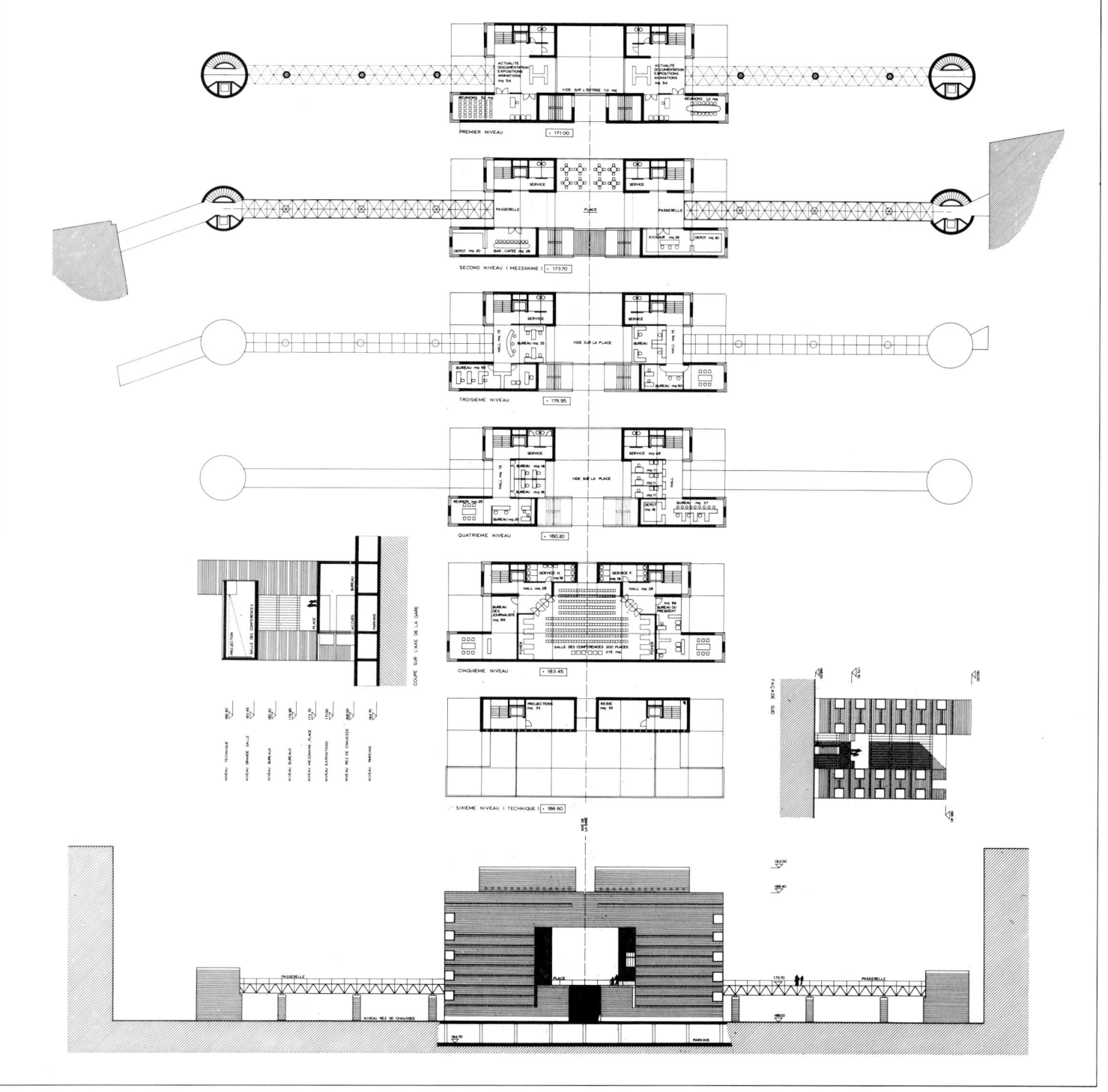

1982 — Project for the new offices of the Bank of Gothard in Lugano, Switzerland

Set in a street of a quarter dating from the beginning of this century, the project subdivides the large building into four blocks so that the street frontage presents alternating solids and voids, setting up a rhythm in proportion to the dimensions of the road. The voids of the four buildings provide spatial and visual relationship between the different levels for banking administration on the upper floors. The ground floor provides for four different activities.

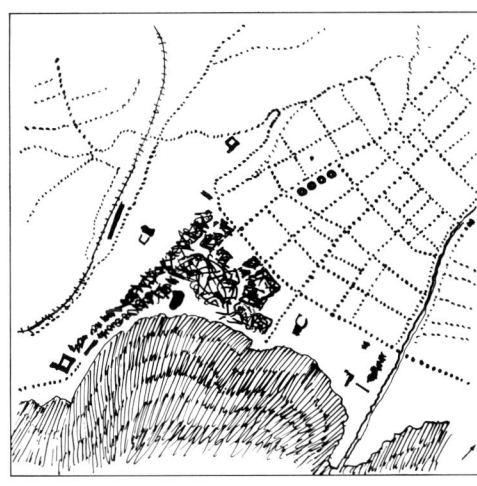

standard floor

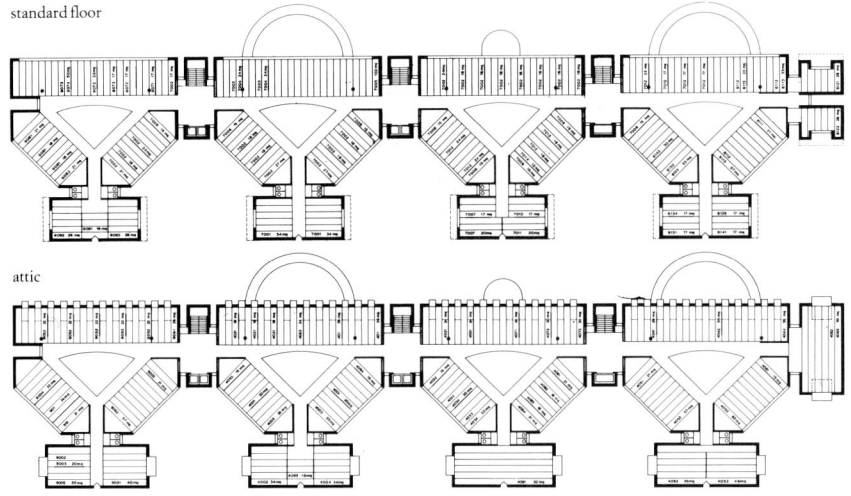

attic

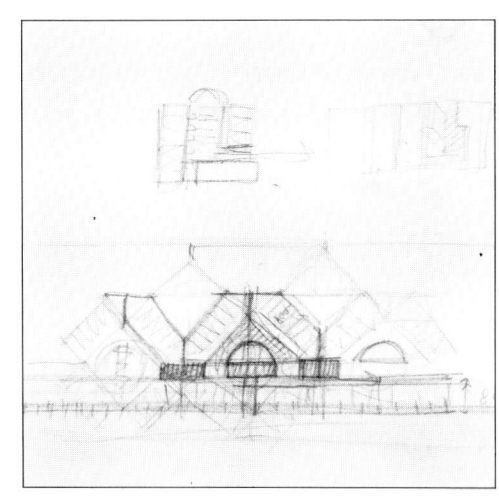

ground floor

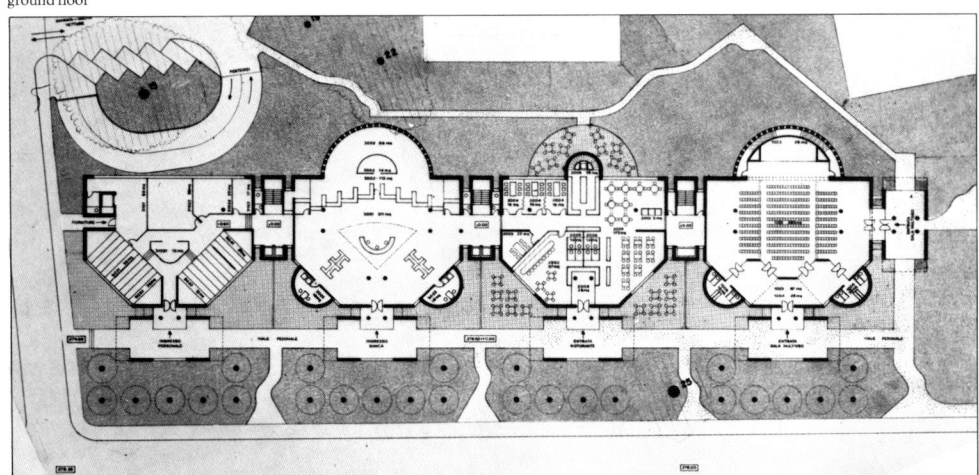

Large-scale projects

1970

Project for a master plan of the new Lausanne Polytechnic, Switzerland
with Tita Carloni, Aurelio Galfetti, Flora Ruchat, Luigi Snozzi

The object of the project is to produce a master plan capable of translating the schedule of spaces and deadlines into a system of formal spatial relations. This system sets out to allow the widest possible choice within a system of pre-established (spatial, functional, technical, distributive, etc.) relations.

The project right from the start clarifies the relations between the new buildings and their surroundings. Subordinated to these priority choices are the growth and flexibility systems which take place within an established "formal" framework.

The project comprises the following components:

— North-south axis running between two peripheral zones for car parking, it constitutes the project's bearing structure. It is the main collector of pedestrian routes and of energy conduits. The axis is formed by two lateral blades within which the teaching staff's and students' lodgings are housed. Between these two structures are the common services, i.e. entrance, exhibition space, administration, library, restaurant, shops, etc.

— East-west axis stretches between the external car parks to the east and west of the area. It forms the teaching axis along which are the auditoriums, seminar halls, lecture-room, etc. It divides the "industrial landscape" of the north zone from the large space which opens towards the city and the lake.

— The square forms the perimeter inside which the various departments, with their own distribution and growth are aggregated to one another. The vertical connections are the fixed planning elements.

— The "halles" sized as industrial equipment, these are organized in line as parallel structures in the northern sector where they benefit from a vehicular system of their own.

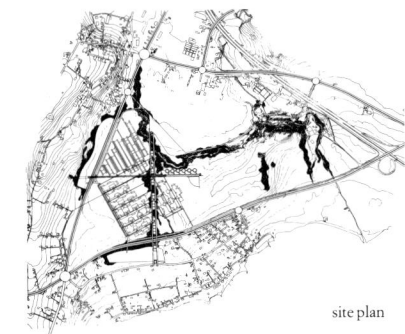

site plan

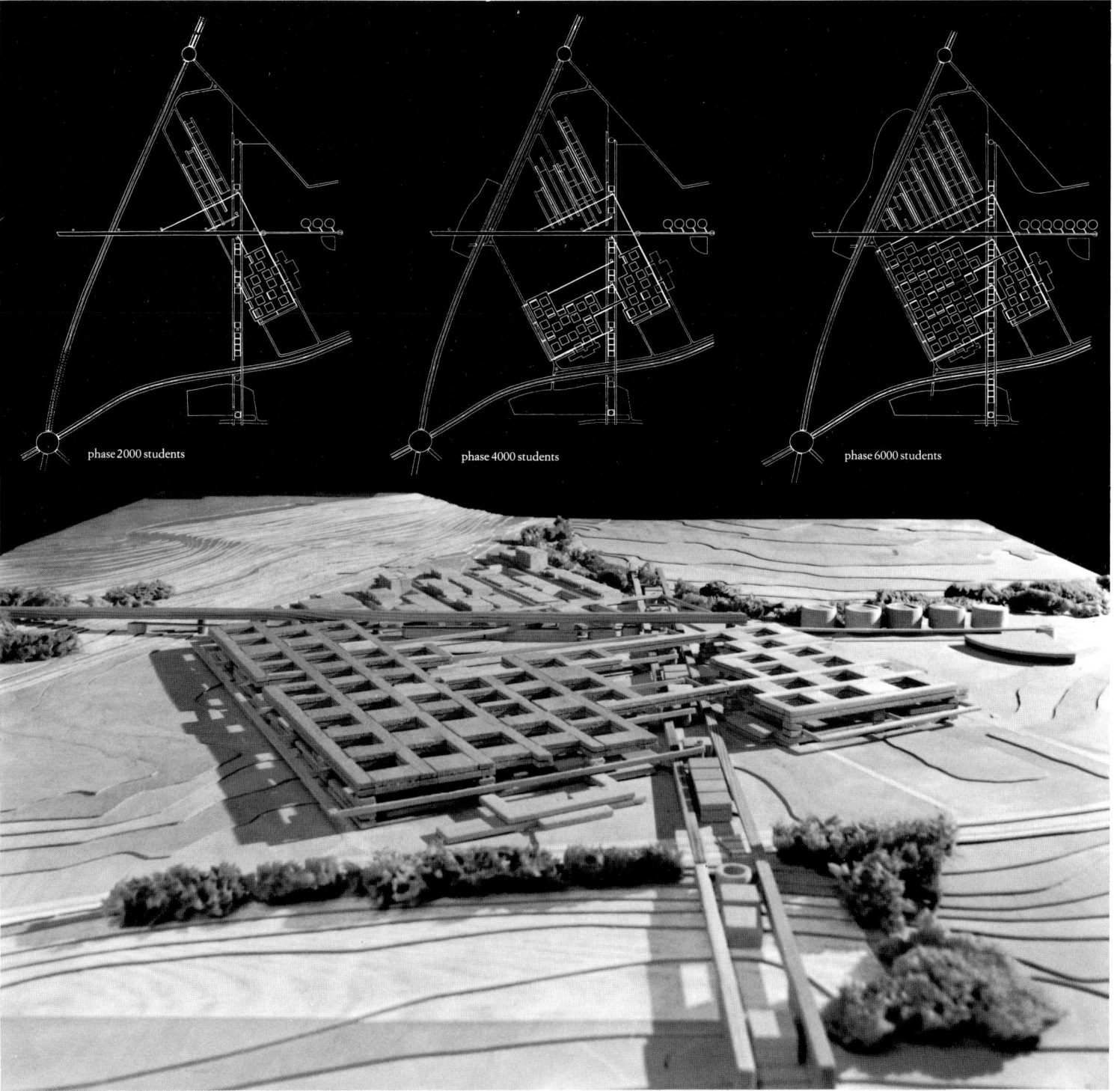

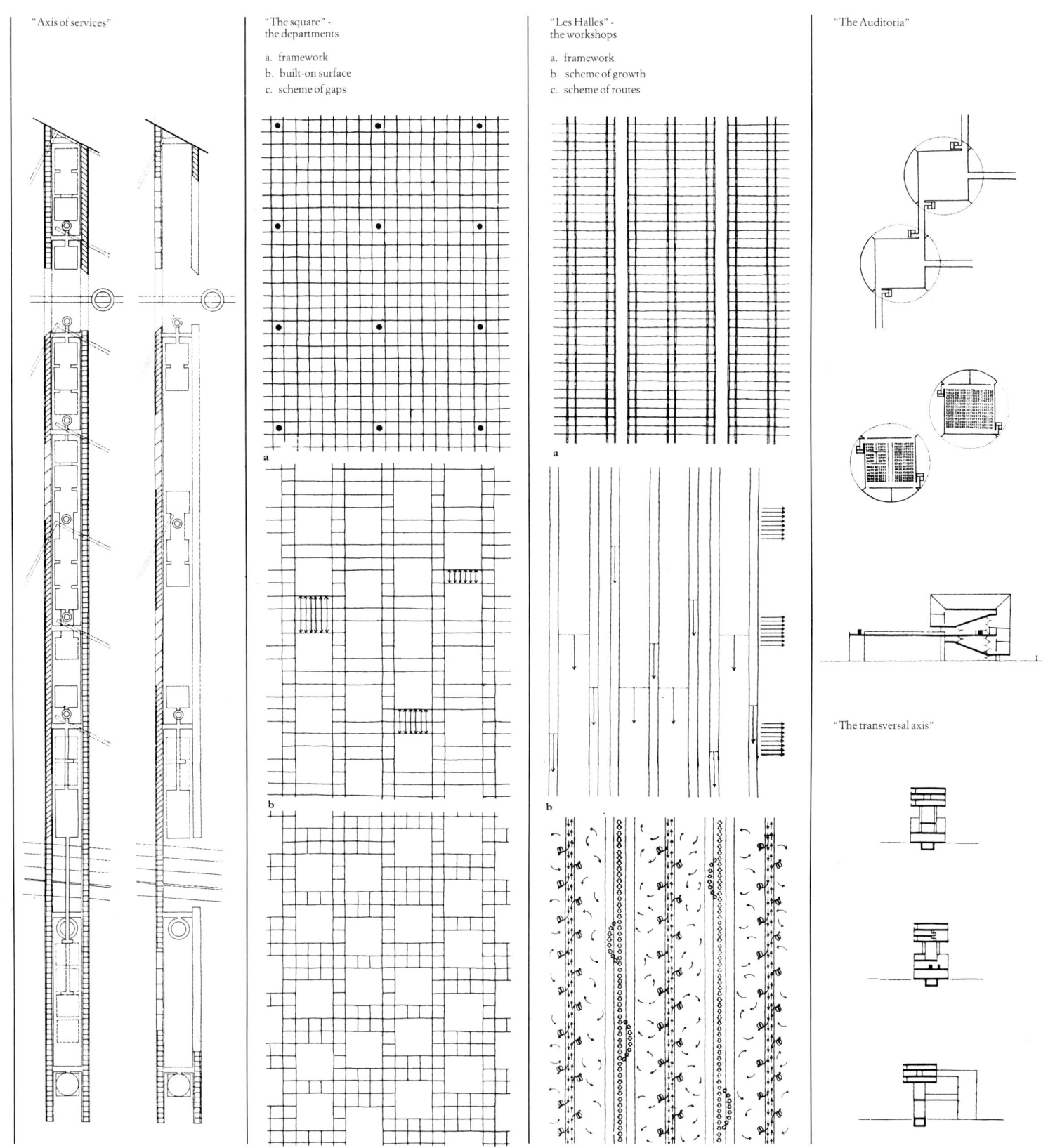

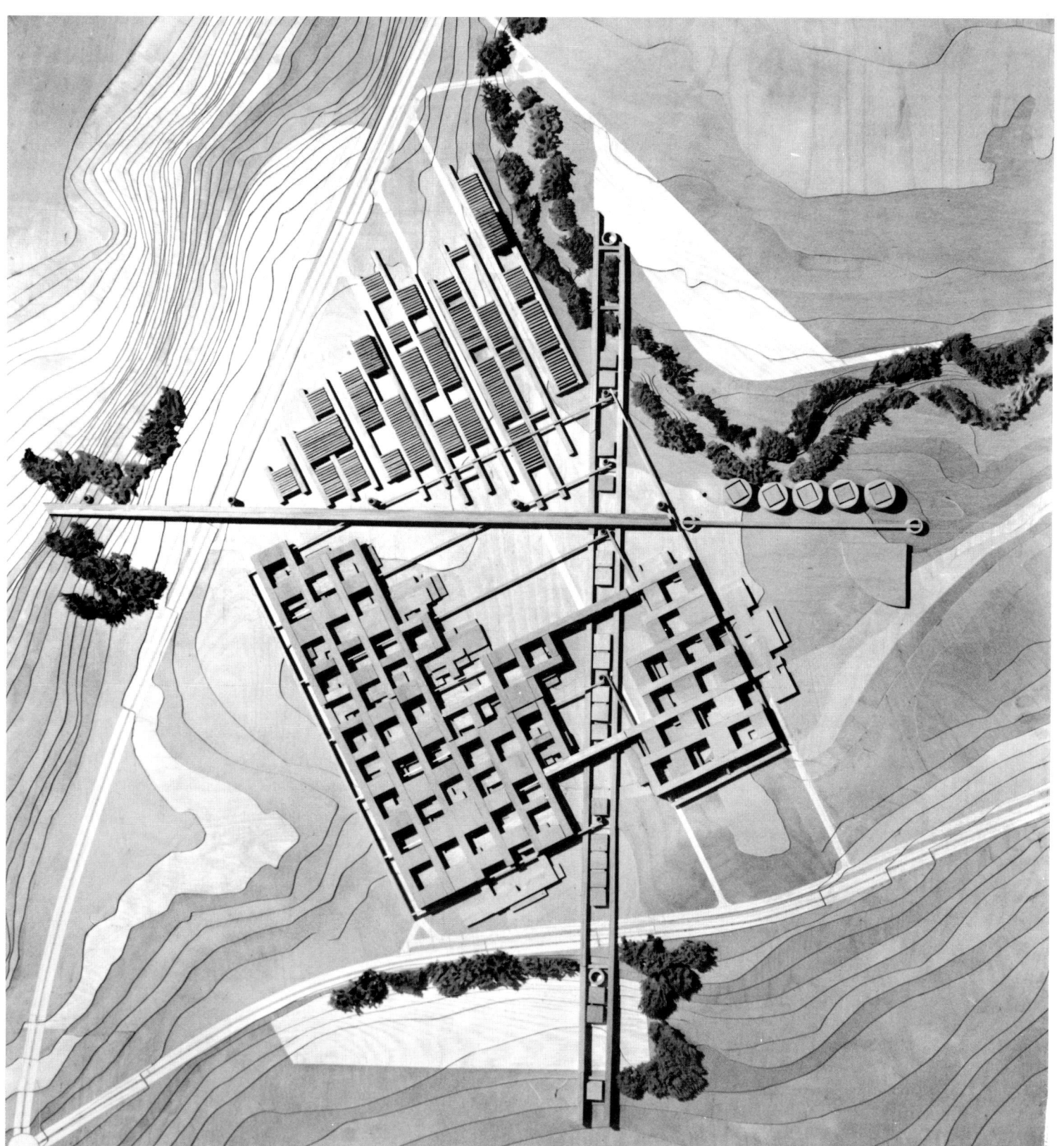

1971

Competition for the new administrative center in Perugia, Italy
with Luigi Snozzi

The proposed design was prepared within the restrictions and limits specified by the competition announcement and by the planning scheme. These limits were explicitly adopted as real data in an existing situation, as parameters to explain the present contradictions with which the territory is organized and directed.
Our objectives were:
The formation of a "primary structure" (the administrative spine) of an alternative urban space contrasting with the ratio of solid volumes and empty spaces proposed by the restructuring planned around it.
Definition of free spaces as "designed" parts in the city and not as spaces left over from the constructed volumes.
Separation and characterization according to different scales of vehicular traffic and of pedestrian ways.
The creation of a system of relation between the historic city and the administrative area (seen as animating poles of the new urban agglomeration) which, apart from its functional transport purpose, will also offer the population a fresh appreciation of the urban landscape.
The project comprises four principal operations: the axis of the administrative spine, the diagonal structure of the municipal offices, the housing quadrilateral, the park.

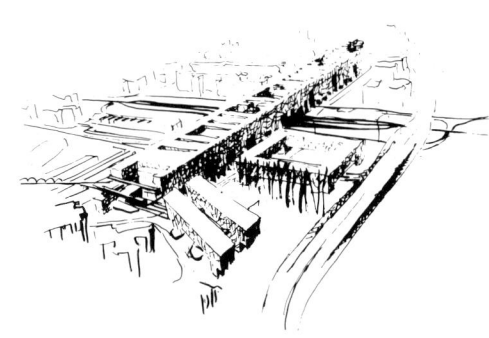

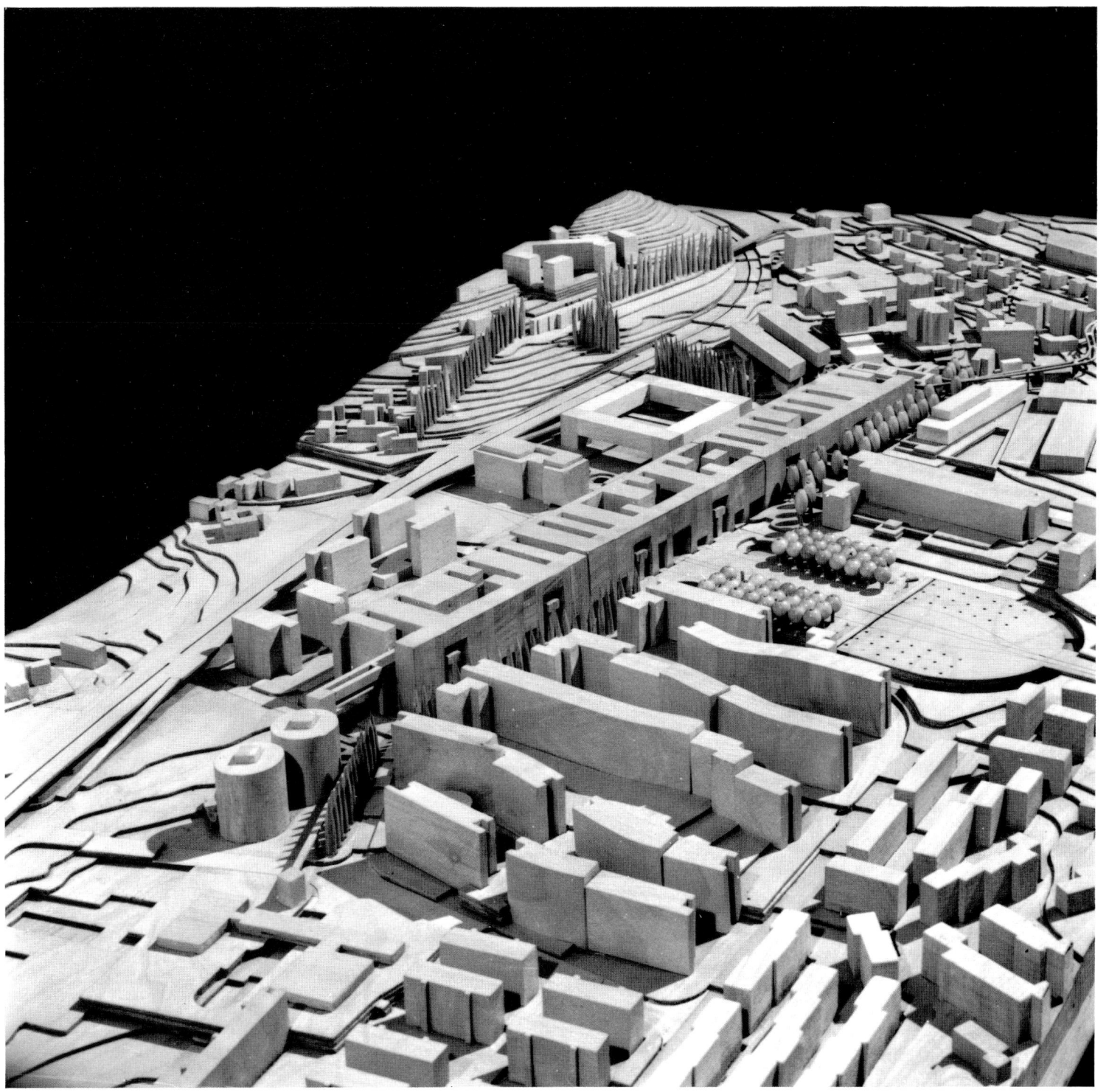

1974

Competition for a housing estate in Mendrisio, Switzerland

with Luigi Snozzi

The land proposed for this residential area is situated on the lowest slopes of Monte San Giorgio, above the flat San Martino zone and on the motorway exit for Mendrisio on the north-south Gothard-Milan stretch.
The project proposed:
The formation, to the south of the area, of a broad green space between the natural wooded profile delimiting the slopes below and the new vehicular access road to the new complex uphill.
The housing estate, grouped within a compact fabric uphill from the old farmhouse.
The built fabric configured around a broad square with the intention of checking the space surrounding the old farmhouse, thereby giving it the quality of a fulcrum.
Using the existing farmhouse as a historico-environmental landmark, the idea being to remove all its strictly functional connotations and to make it the junction of pedestrian ways between the new square and the old pathway leading to the plain below.
The square and its extension northwards form the confluence of all the ways leading to the different homes. A vehicular road for service only describes a ring extending from the terminal at the entrance to the square and joining the existing road further up.
The basic components of the living structure are situated in a progression downhill within a linear system which alternates constructed volumes and empty spaces. The lateral juxtaposition of several elements permits enlargement and growth in successive periods of time.
The constructional element consists of double juxtapositioning of straight masonry structures. The different living cells are organized on three levels with a double orientation towards the valley (east) and towards the mountains (west).
The linear structure of the organizational plan permits an altimetric adaptation to the slope and configuration of the land. The system proposed offers ample scope for distribution of the different dwellings.

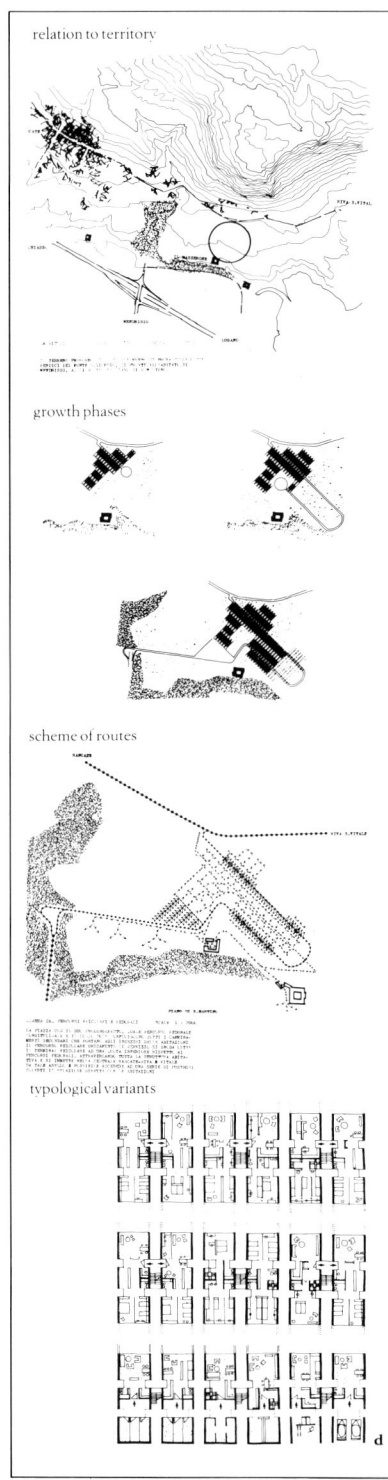

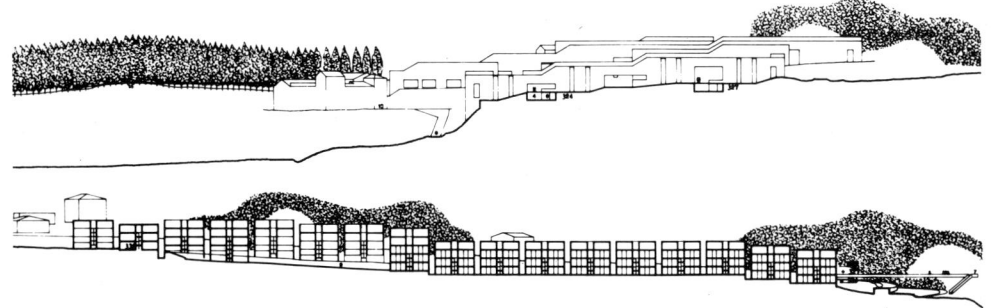

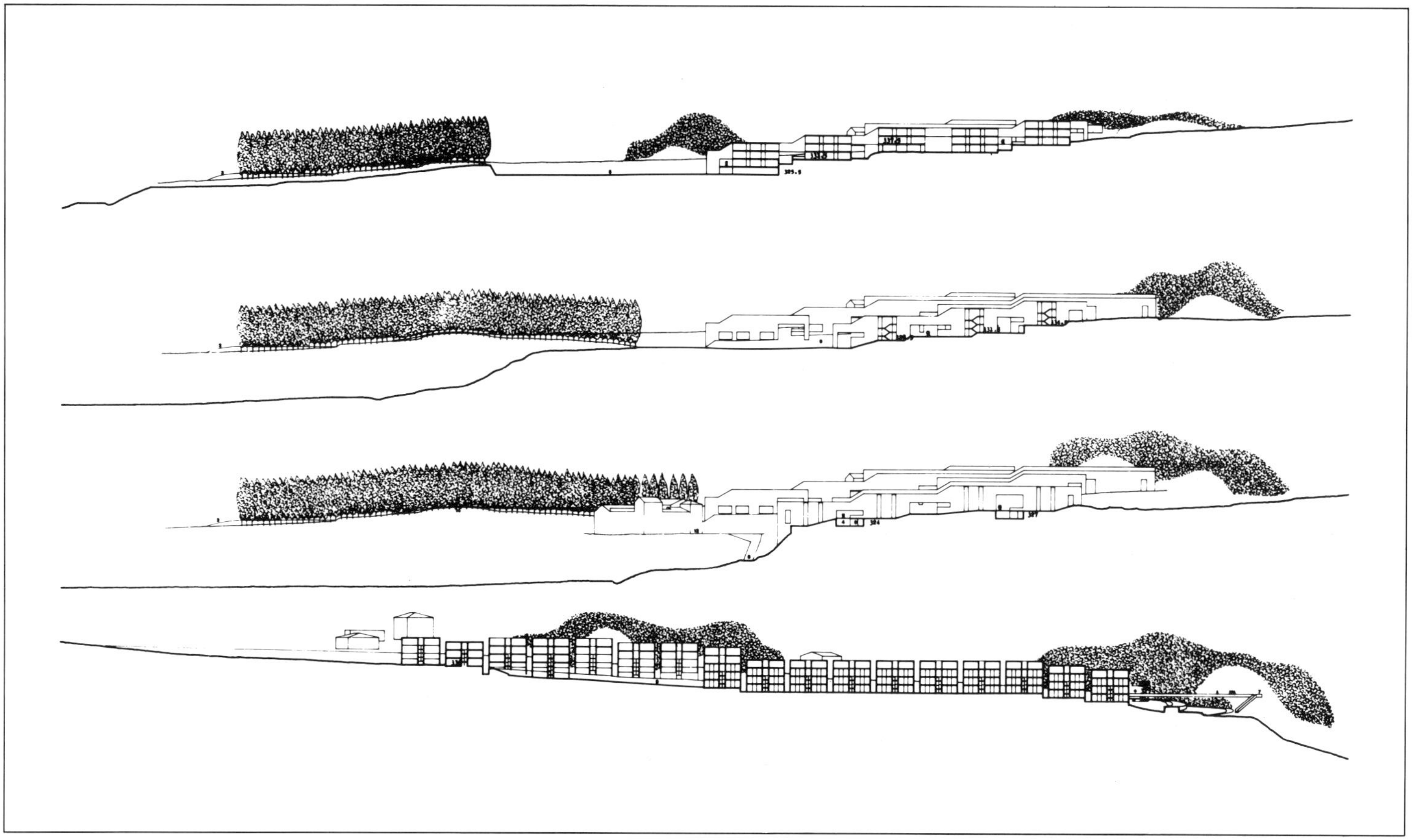

1978

Competition for the enlargement of Zurich station, Switzerland
with Luigi Snozzi

This project for the extension of Zurich station comes as a major opportunity for the spatial and distributive reorganization of an entire district of the city. Prominent among the principal aims is the necessity for a link between two areas of the city which are separated by the railway.
In order to put forward an architectural solution to the questions raised which would also be compatible with our own interpretation of the city, we felt legitimately and, indeed, necessarily bound to remove some of the limits to the operative area indicated in the competition announcement.
The project includes three distinct works: the bridge connecting the Sihlpost to the district lying to the north of the Limmatstrasse, the parking slab, the buildings along the Zollstrasse. The bridge connecting the two districts constitutes a hinge between the existing station and the new enlargement westwards. Its front is aligned with the river Sihl. The height of this new structure echoes the horizon outlined by the Sihlpost building. The two bridge-heads in the project constitute new entrances and junctions between the railways and the surrounding districts.
Situated on different levels around the main longitudinal route of this infrastructure are all the facilities of a public nature specified by the competition announcement, i.e. restaurants, shops, etc. A tree-lined avenue is proposed at roof level to mark a virtual retrieval of the existing trees along the riverside.
The bus and parking slab is to the west of the connecting bridge. Entry to the two vehicular slabs is provided through the Zollstrasse with a system of linear ramps. The two distribution levels (that of the buses on the first floor and that of the car park on the second floor) are connected by foot to the bridge across the railway. Direct connection is thus possible between trains and buses and the car park.
The whole programme of services specified in the announcement is organized along the Zollstrasse. In the urban structure this part of the project is located in the residential spaces existing between the railway and the town. On the one hand it aims to define clearly the space and the railway area in respect to the city, and on the other, to complete and re-enliven the entire district facing the Zollstrasse. This operation proposes a typology characterized by a "wall" — as a defence against noise — along the railway, and by a series of buildings facing east-west towards the street.

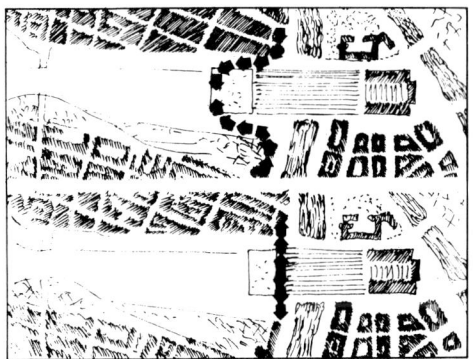

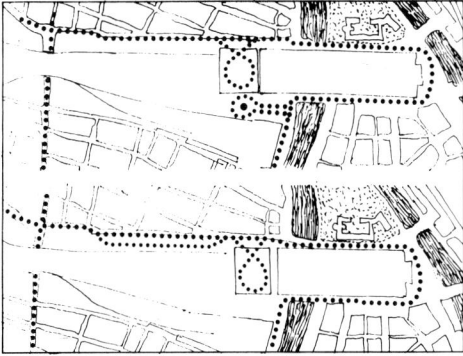

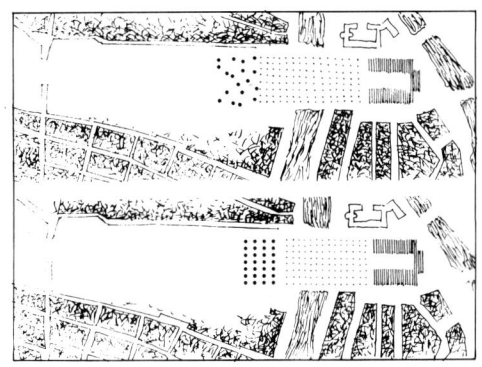

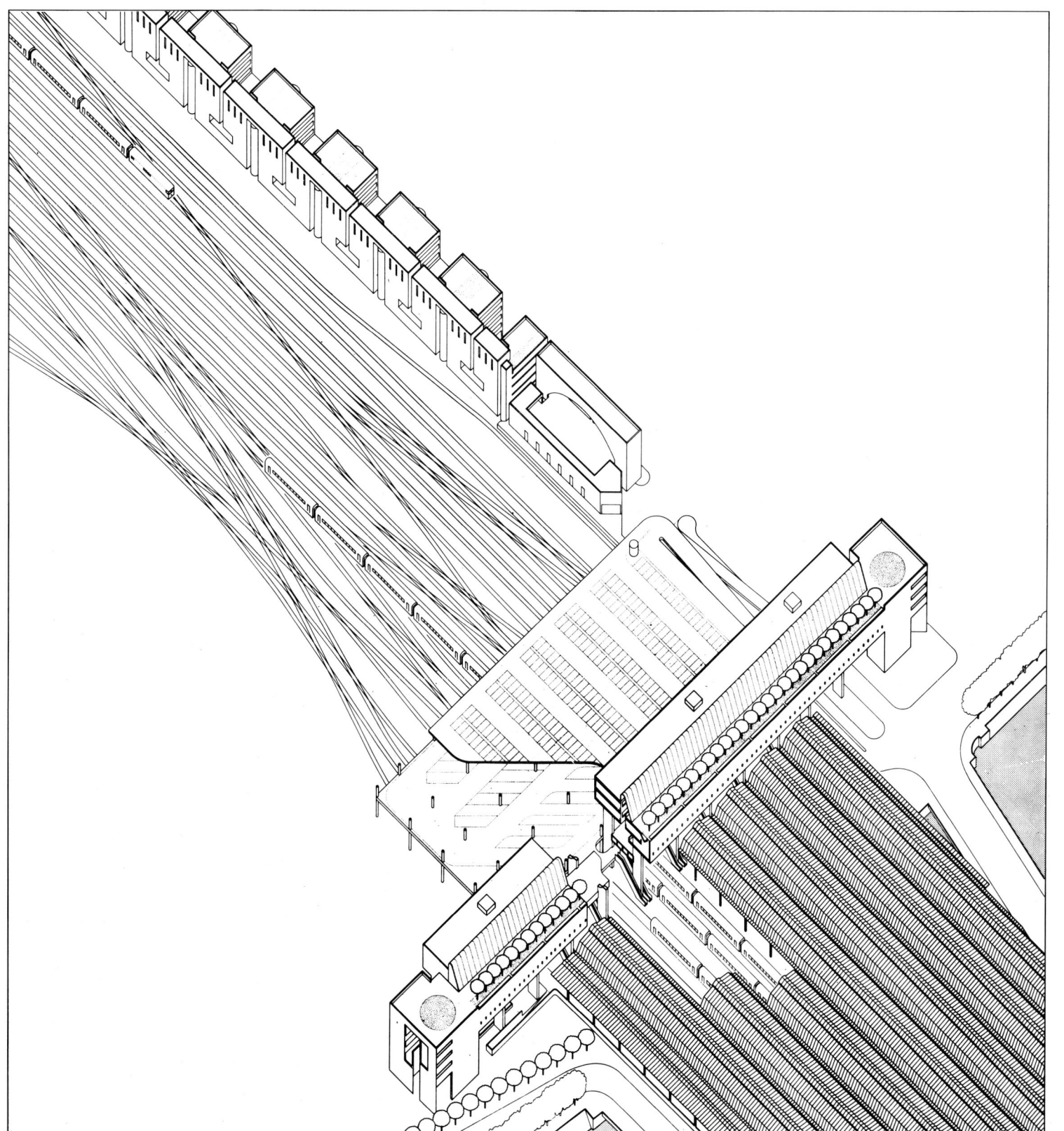

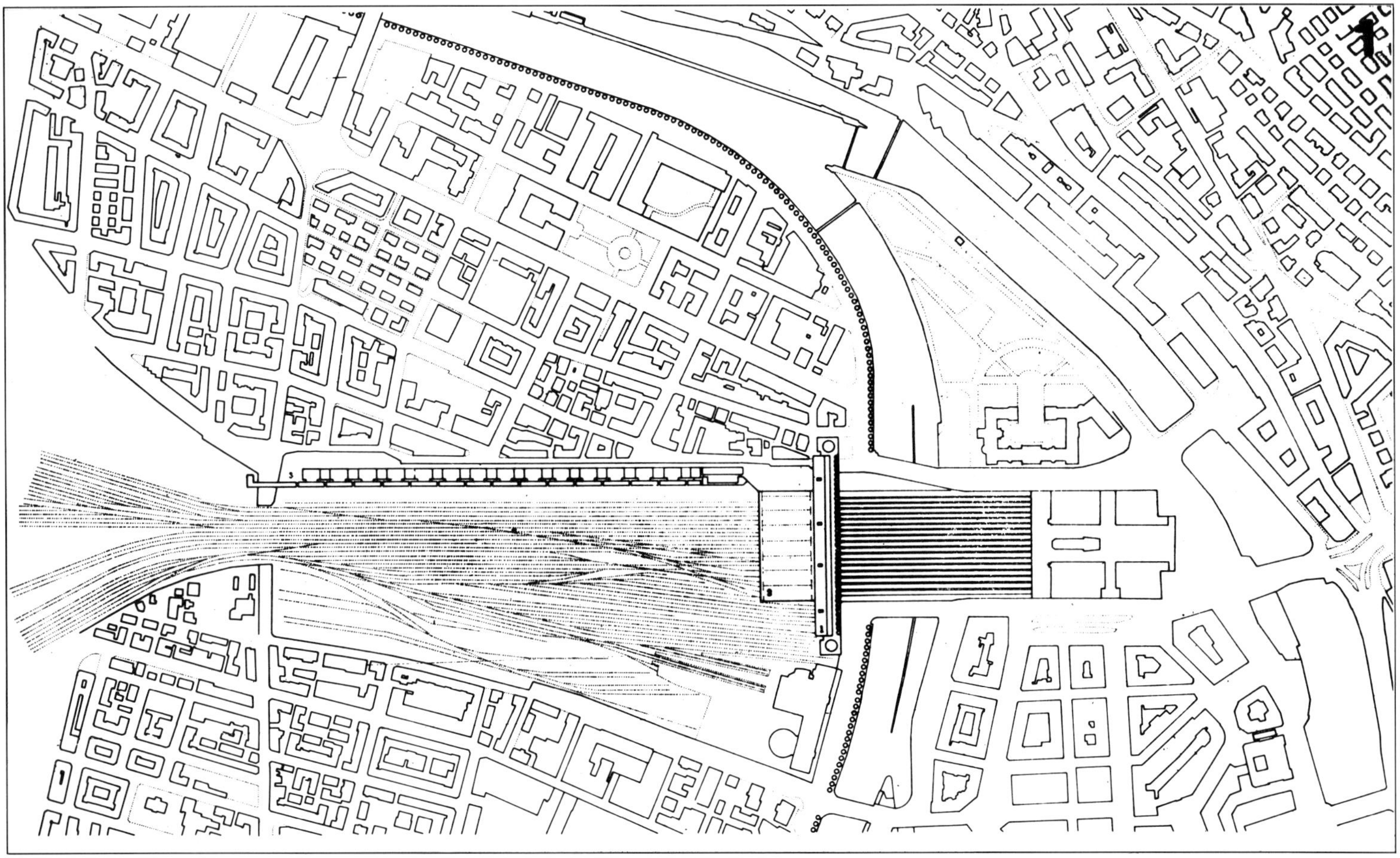

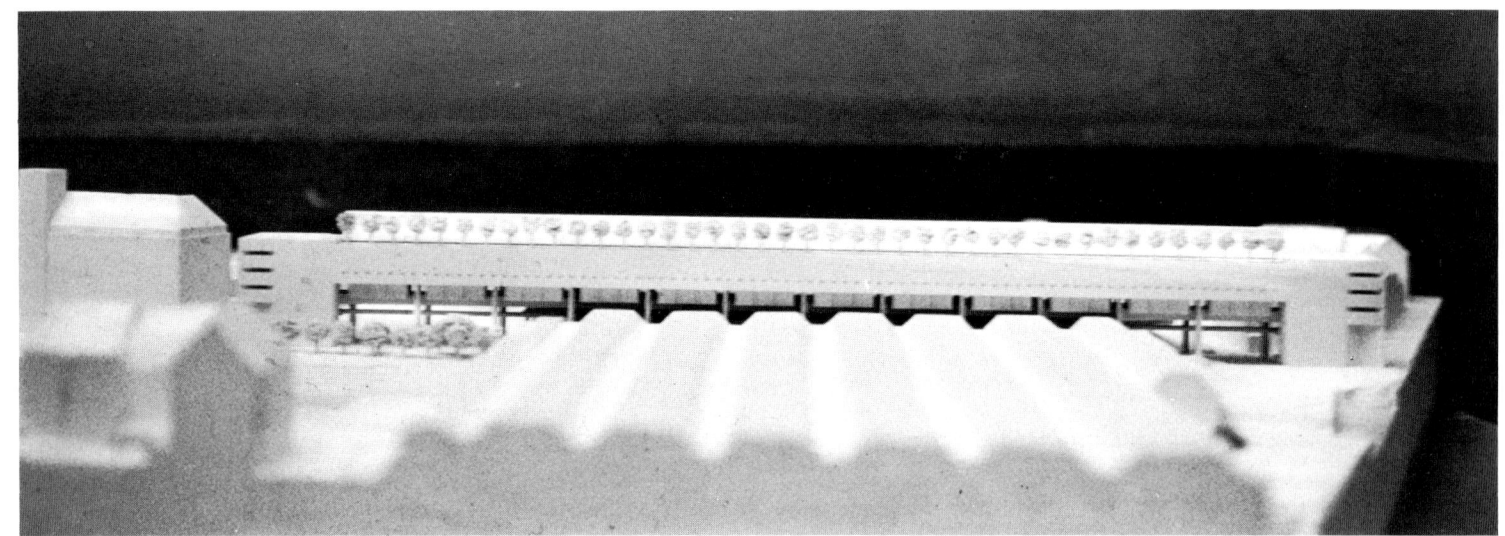

The bridge
a. plan on railway level
b. plan on bus station level
c. plan on parking level
d. elevation along the river, access blocks and sections

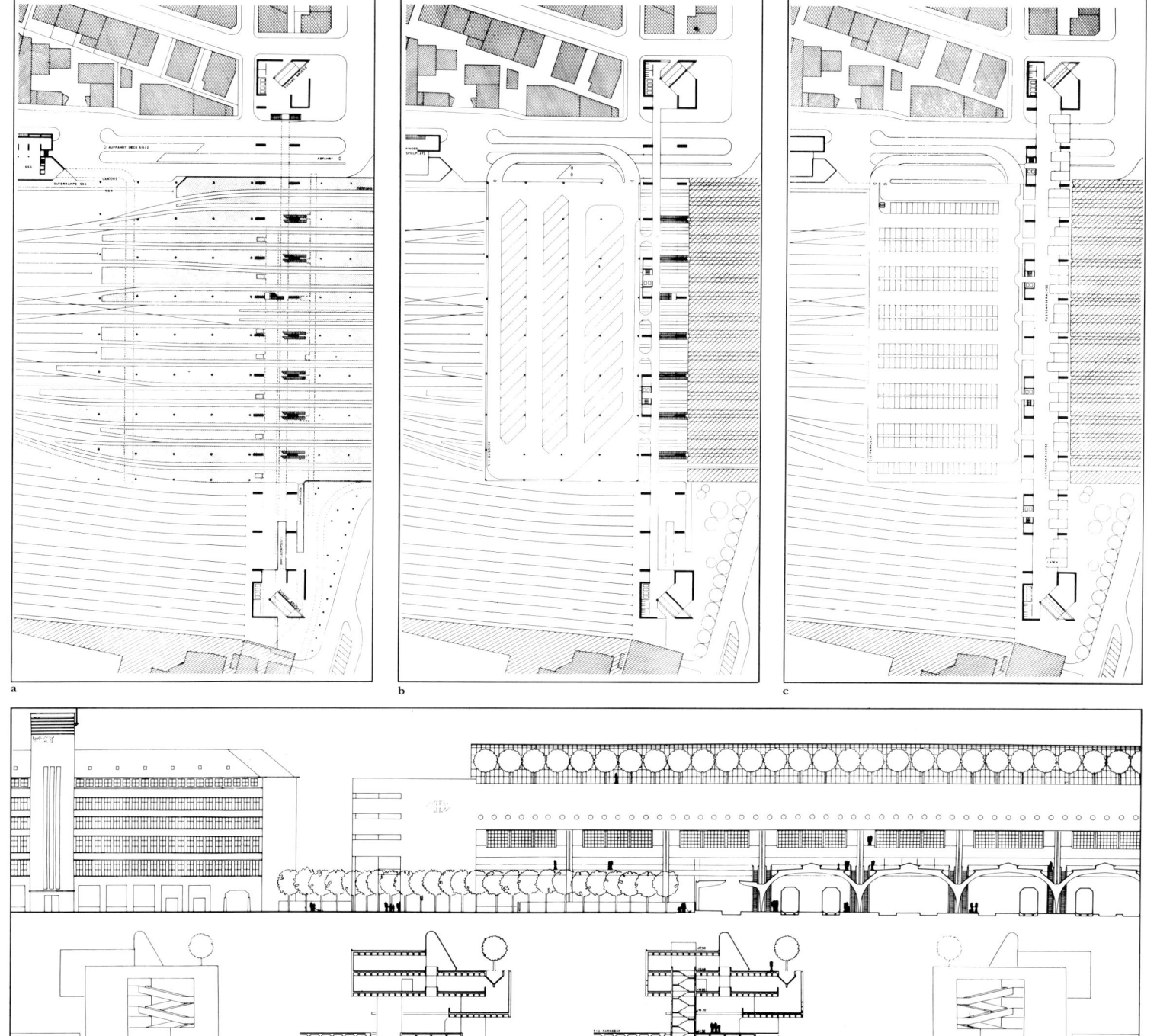

Buildings along the Zollstrasse
a. ground floor
b. second floor
c. d. upper levels
e. elevation on the Zollstrasse
f. sections
g. elevation on the railway

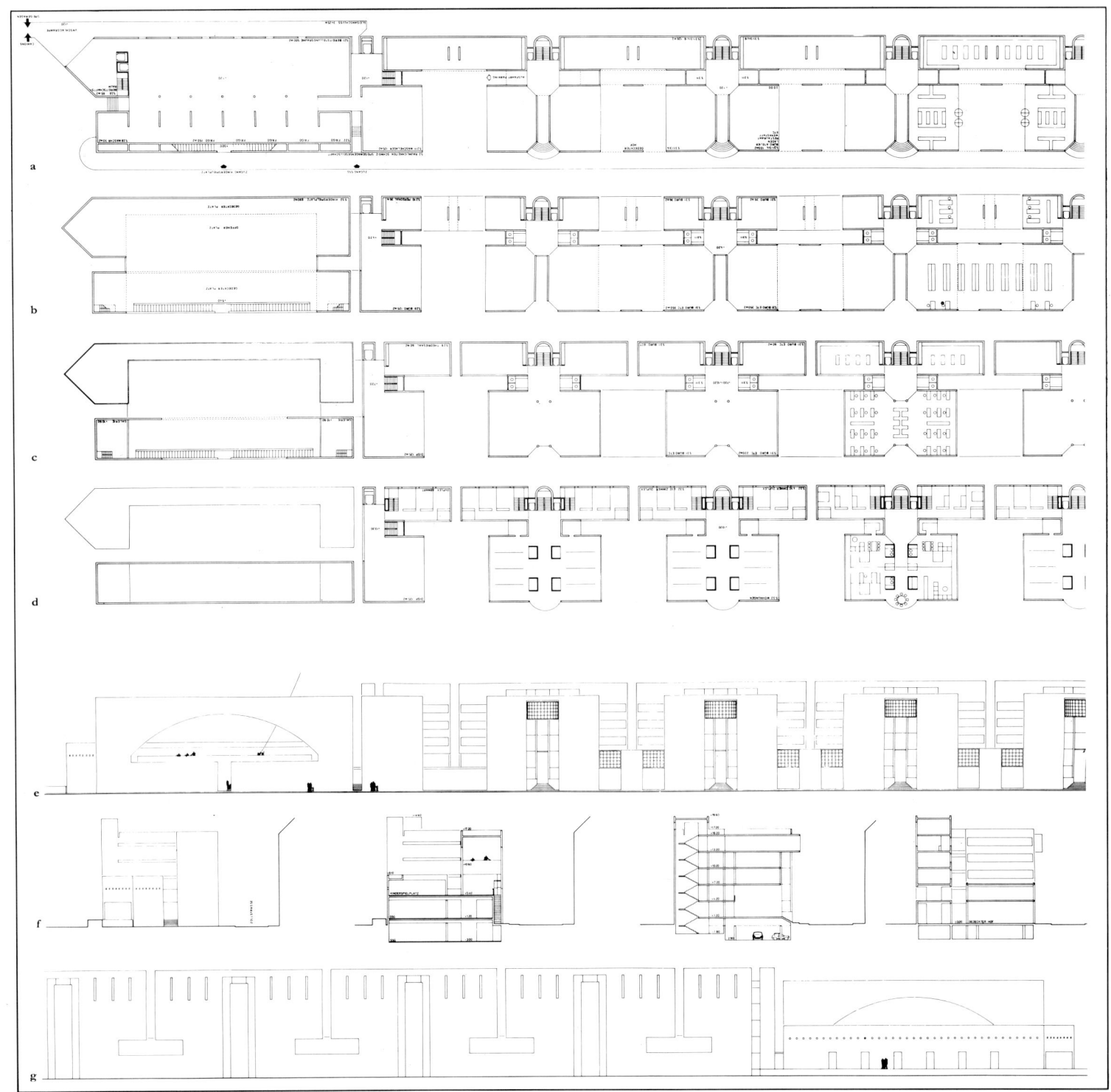

Proposals compared
(1 programme, 2 project)
a. link between the two quarters
b. scheme of traffic
c. static system

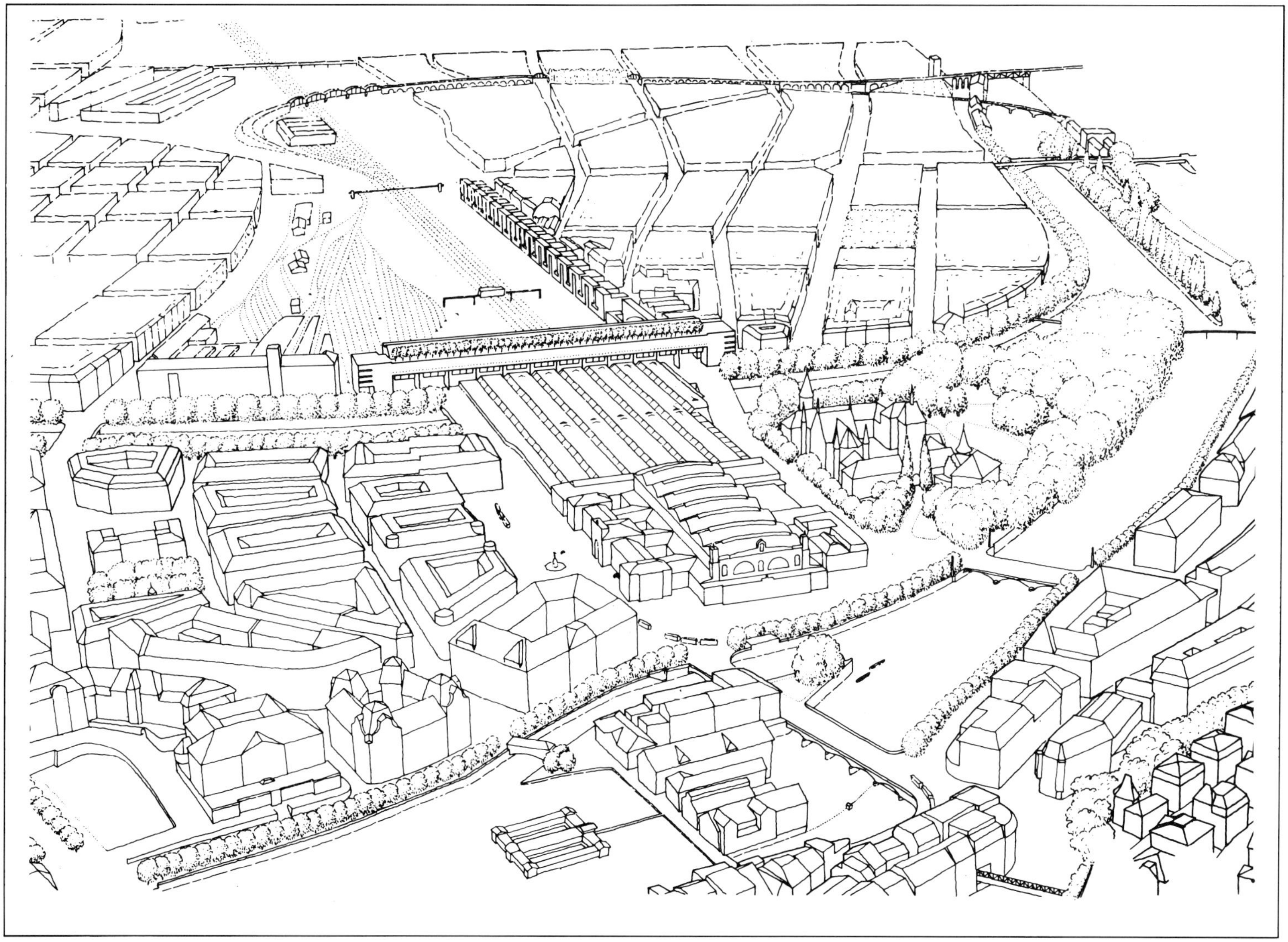

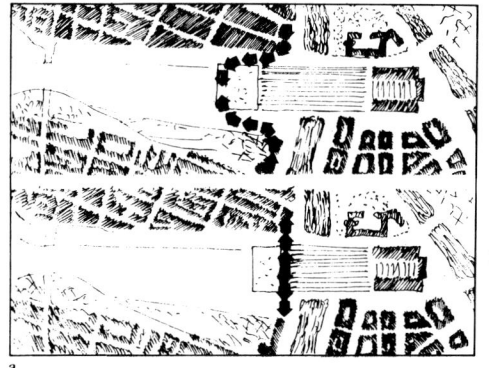
a

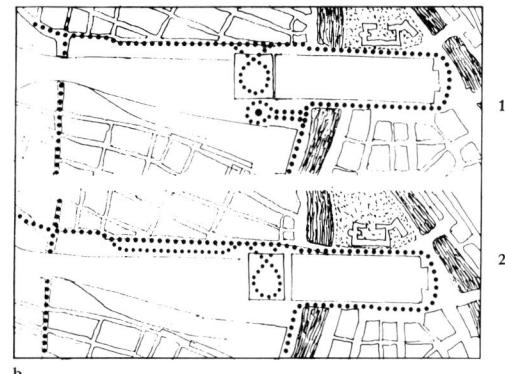
b

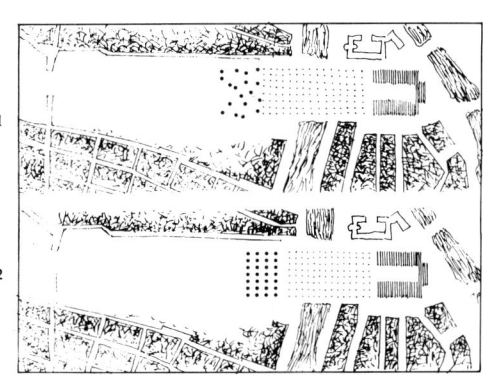
c

1979

Competition for the redevelopment of an area in Basel, Switzerland

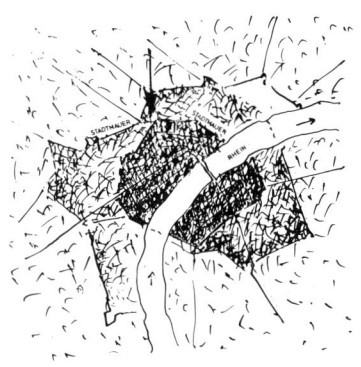

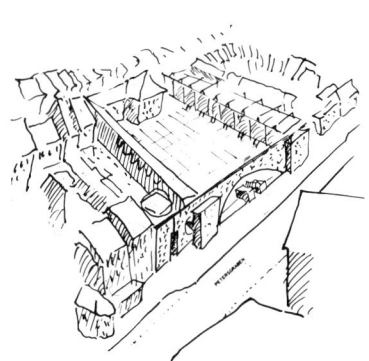

The competition was for an area on the inner limit of the old walled town currently used for parking scheduled for redevelopment. The competition announcement specifies housing, a car park and possible district services.
The objectives of the project are definition of this area as a boundary between the compact mediaeval fabric of the historic town and that of the looser building which has grown up outside the old city walls.
Our operative criteria are: the formation of a building fabric with adjacent housing on the south front with a view to re-establishing the original balance of spaces; proposal for dwellings organized on two levels with distribution routes on the ground and second floors; the formation of a backcloth-wall along the line of the old walls, the idea being spatially to control the courtyard area in respect to the external building fabric. It is a "physical" transitional structure between the two building fabrics. The formation of an underground car park in the courtyard area (ex-nineteenth century garden). Its roofing is a square with trees planted in mobile containers upon it.

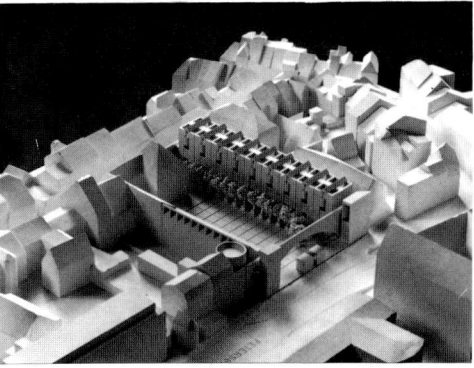

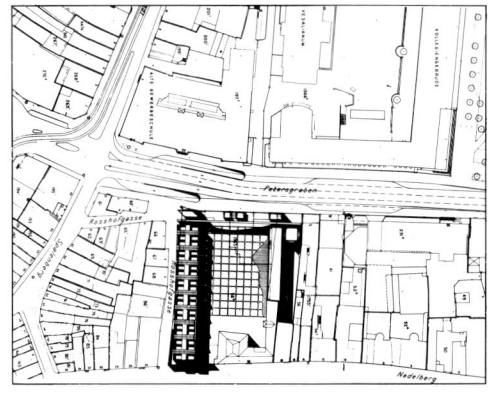

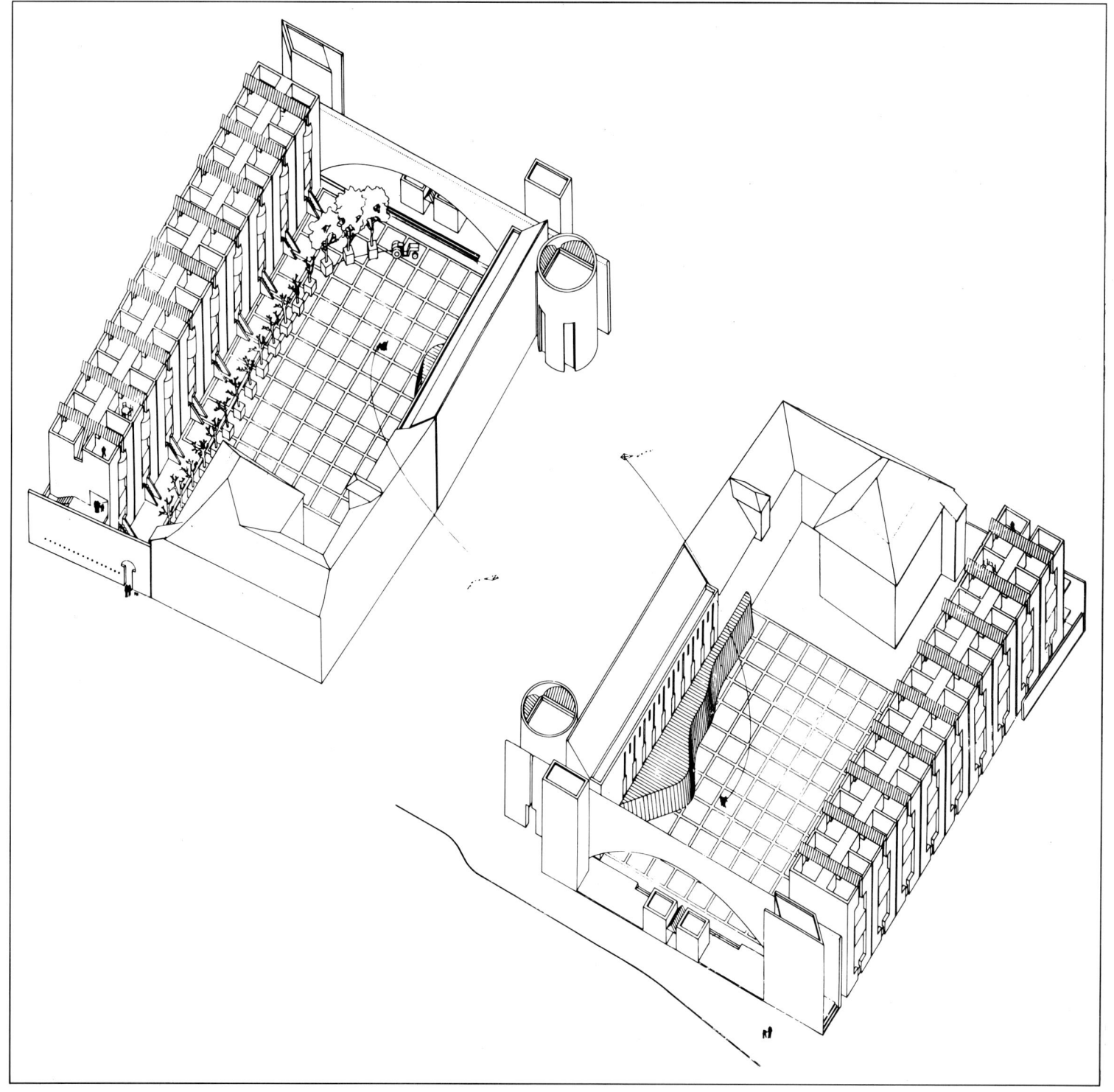

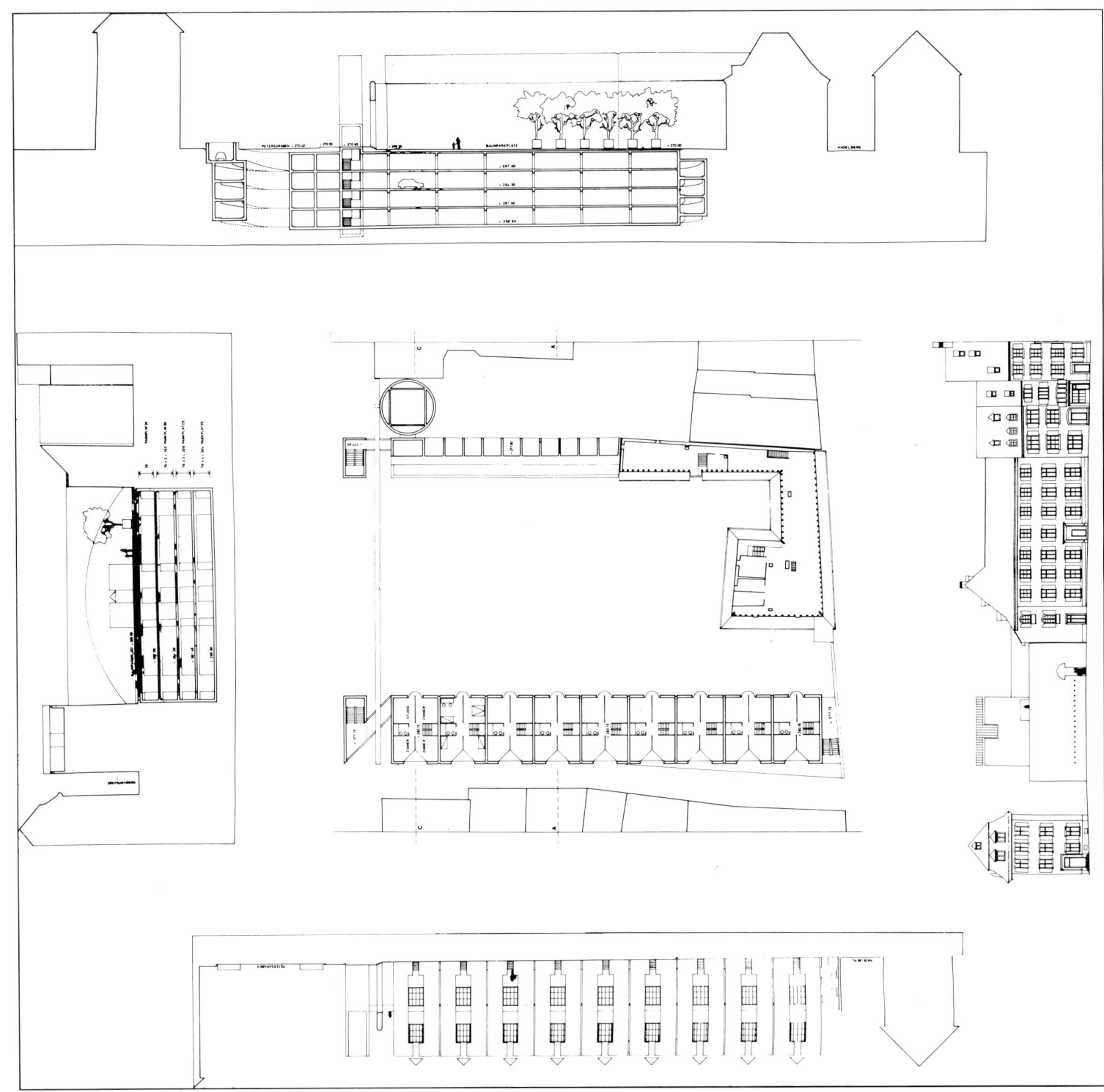

a. ground floor
b. second floor
c. third floor
d. roofing

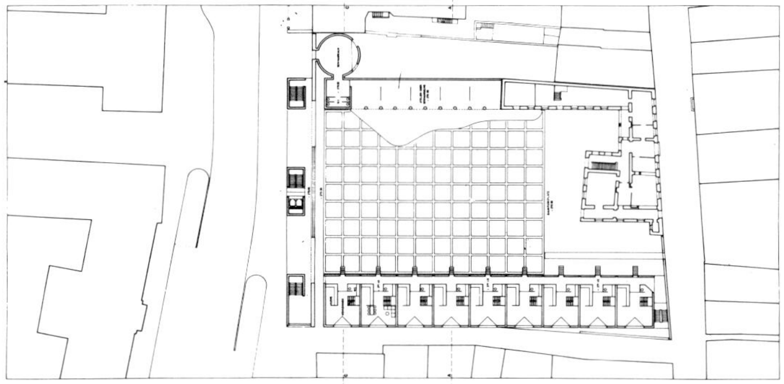
a

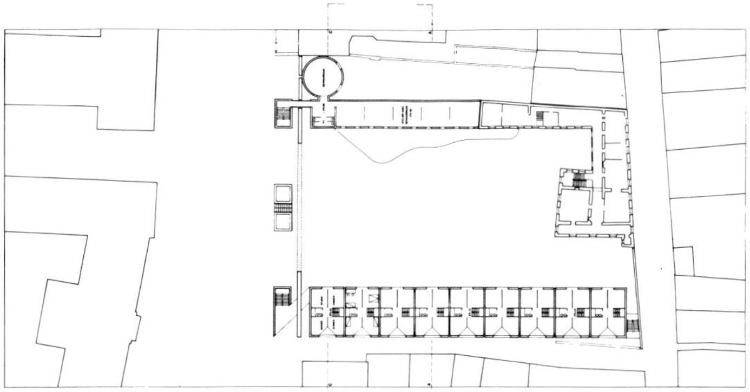
b

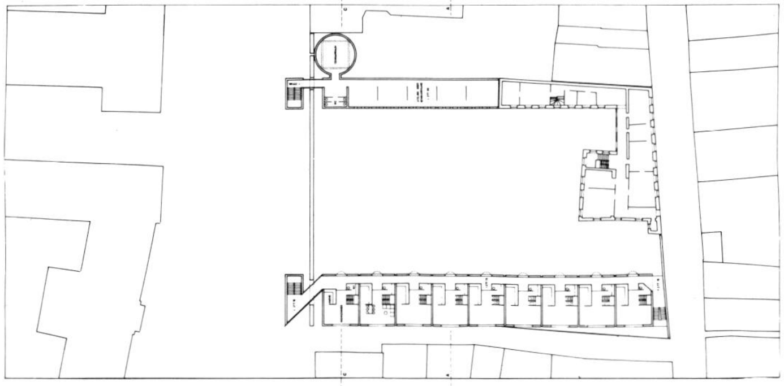
c

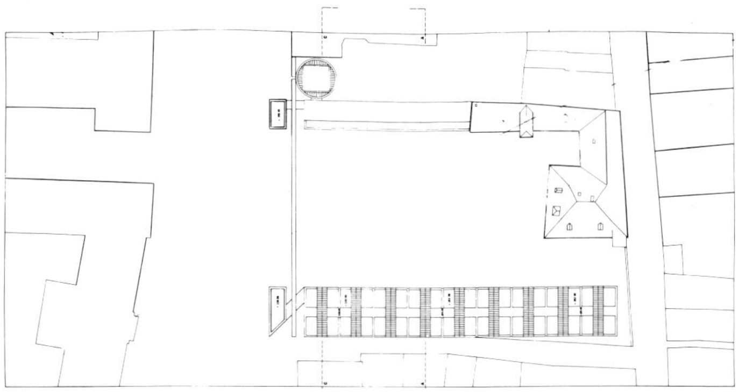
d

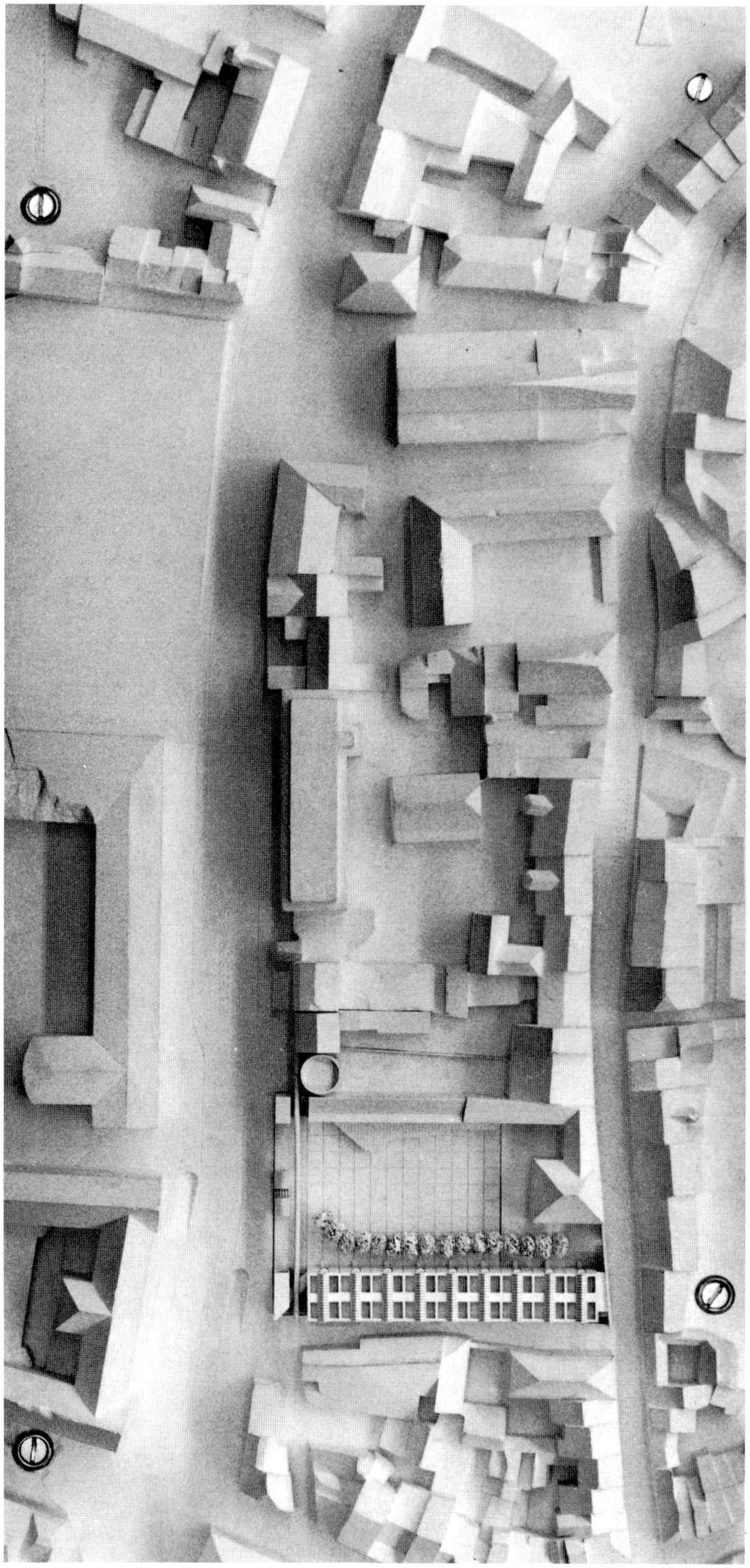

1980 **Project for a lake-side recreational area in Lugano, Switzerland**

An examination of the site led to the suggestion that the land provided, which extends down to the lake, should only be built up in such a way as to leave open spaces.
The required facilities have therefore been gathered where they are in rapport with and closer to the town and its fabric.
The different activities (tennis, bathing and the harbor) are in sectors divided by rows of trees. A tree floats on the water and marks the geometric recomposition of the tree lines.

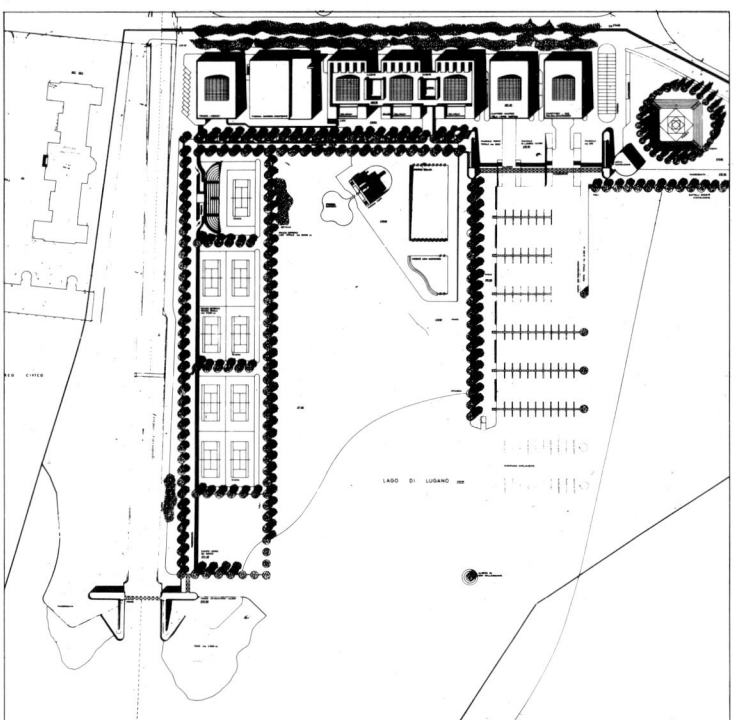
present state

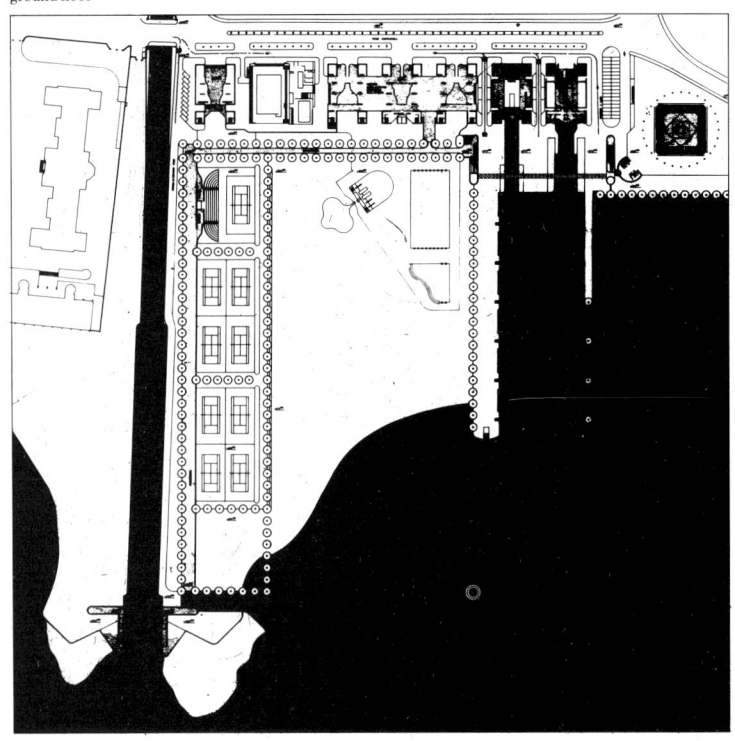
ground floor

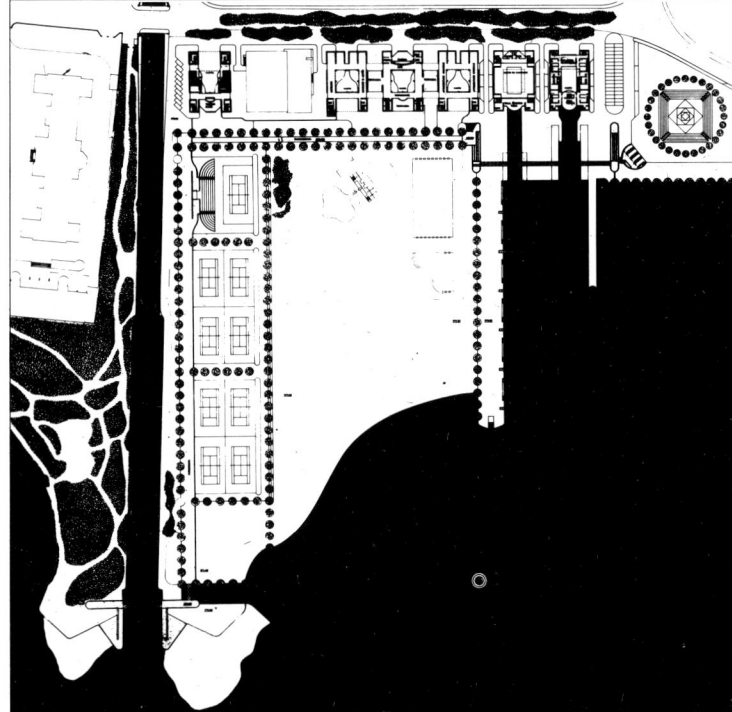
second floor

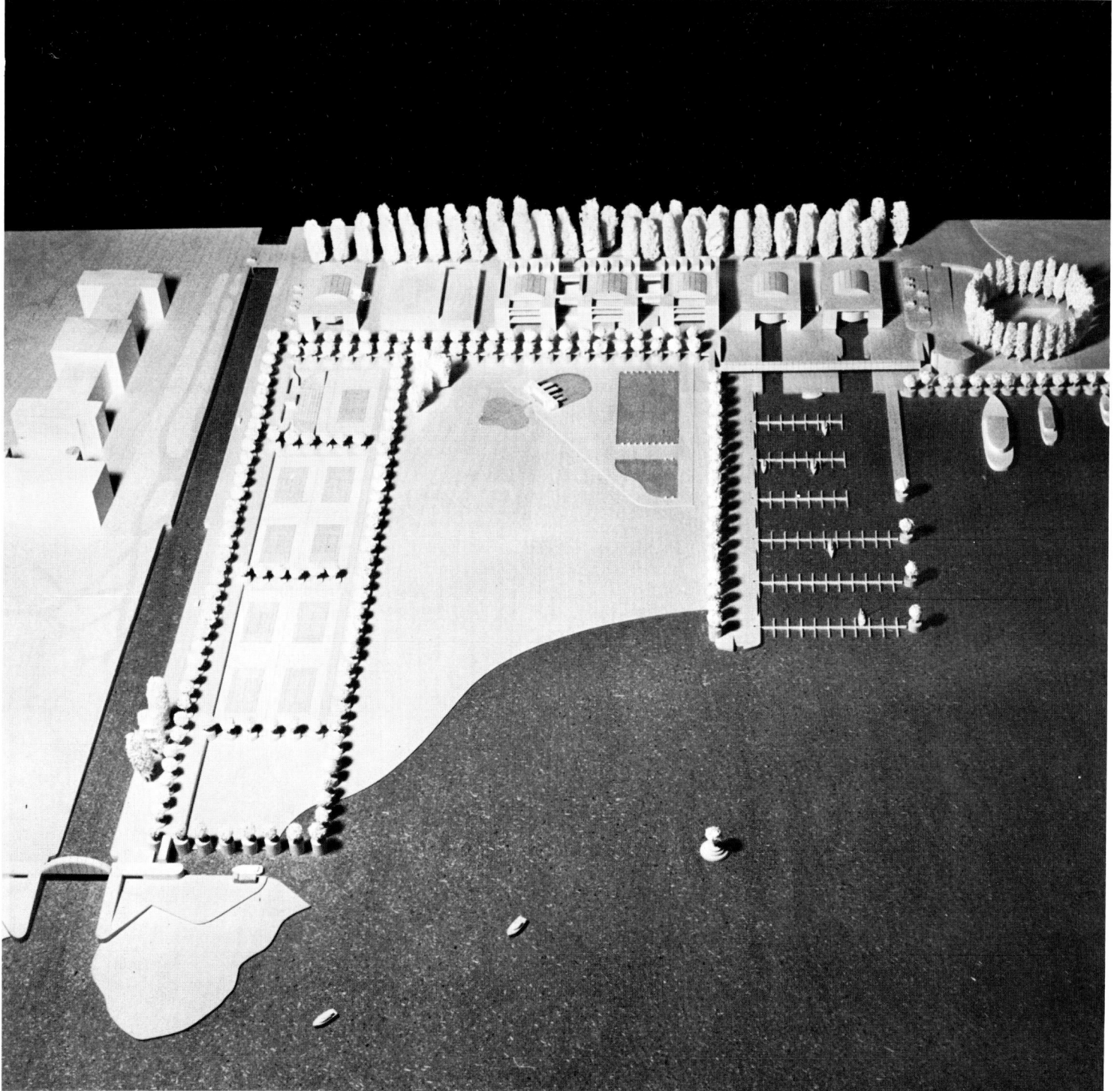

1980   **Competition for a science center in Berlin, West Germany**

This project was entered for a competition held by the Internationale Bauausstellung Berlin 1984 for the construction of a science center, is to be situated between the National Gallery of Modern Art (Mies van der Rohe, 1968) to the east and the Schellhaus (Fahrenkamp, 1931) to the west. The new complex should have a functional relationship with the existing building that faces the Landwehrkanal.

The project envisages construction on the perimeter, thus reinforcing the idea of urban fabric around the canal, in contrast to the tendency to prefer isolated interventions within an indefinite fabric that appeared in this sector during the sixties and seventies.

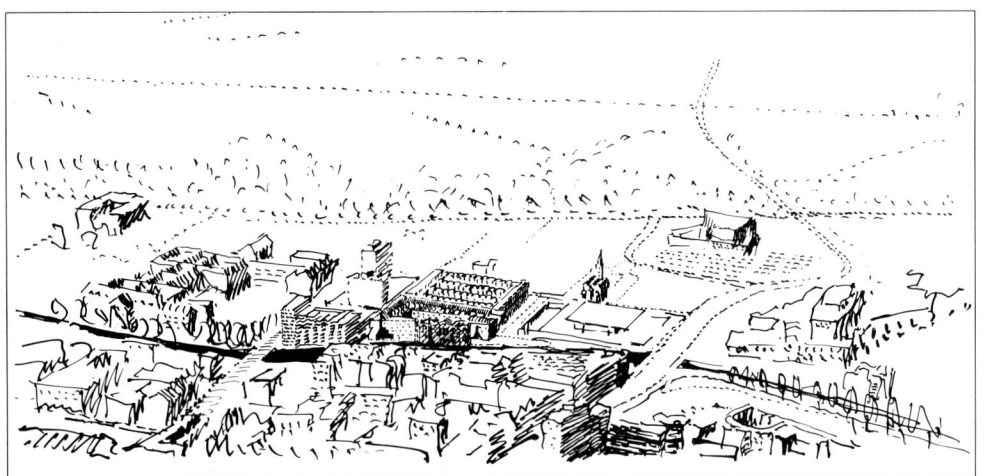

 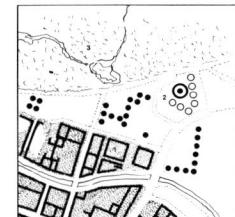
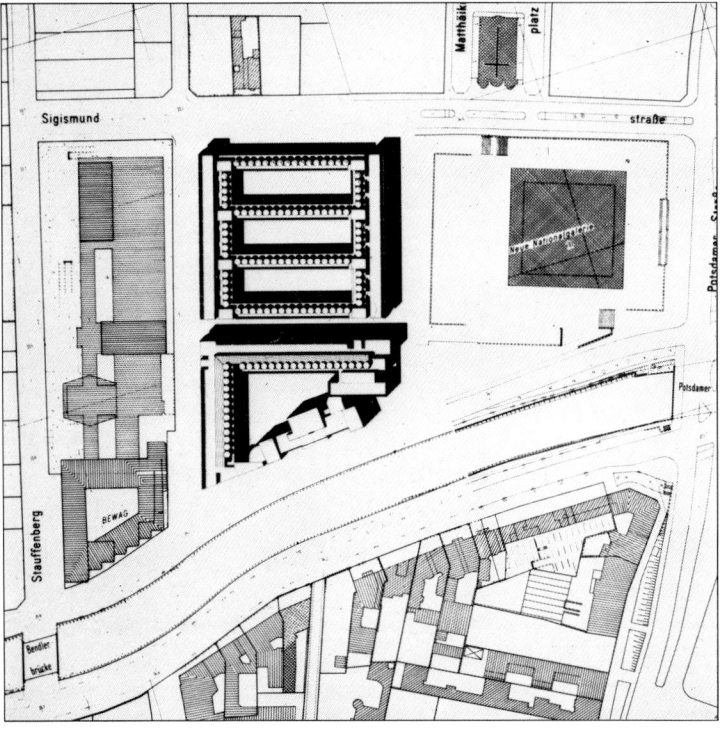 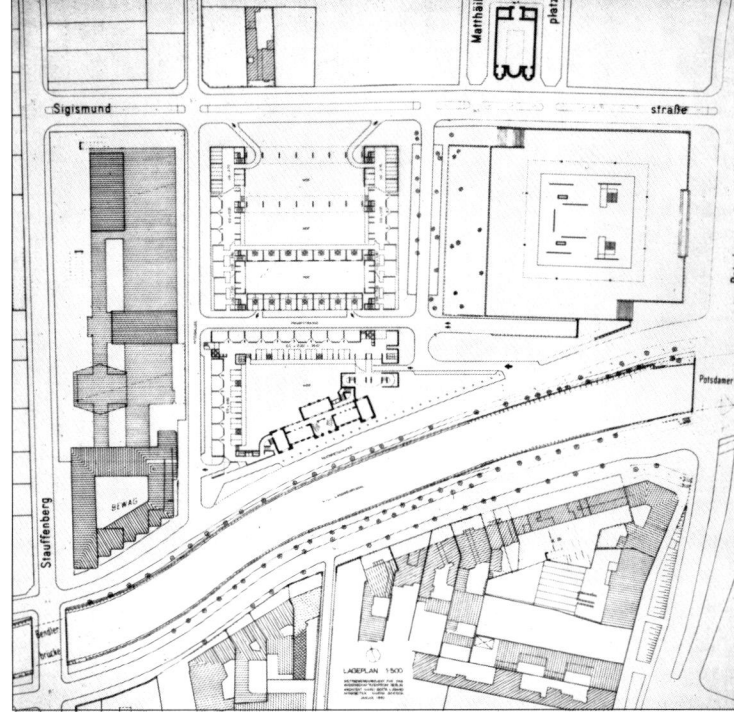

ground floor

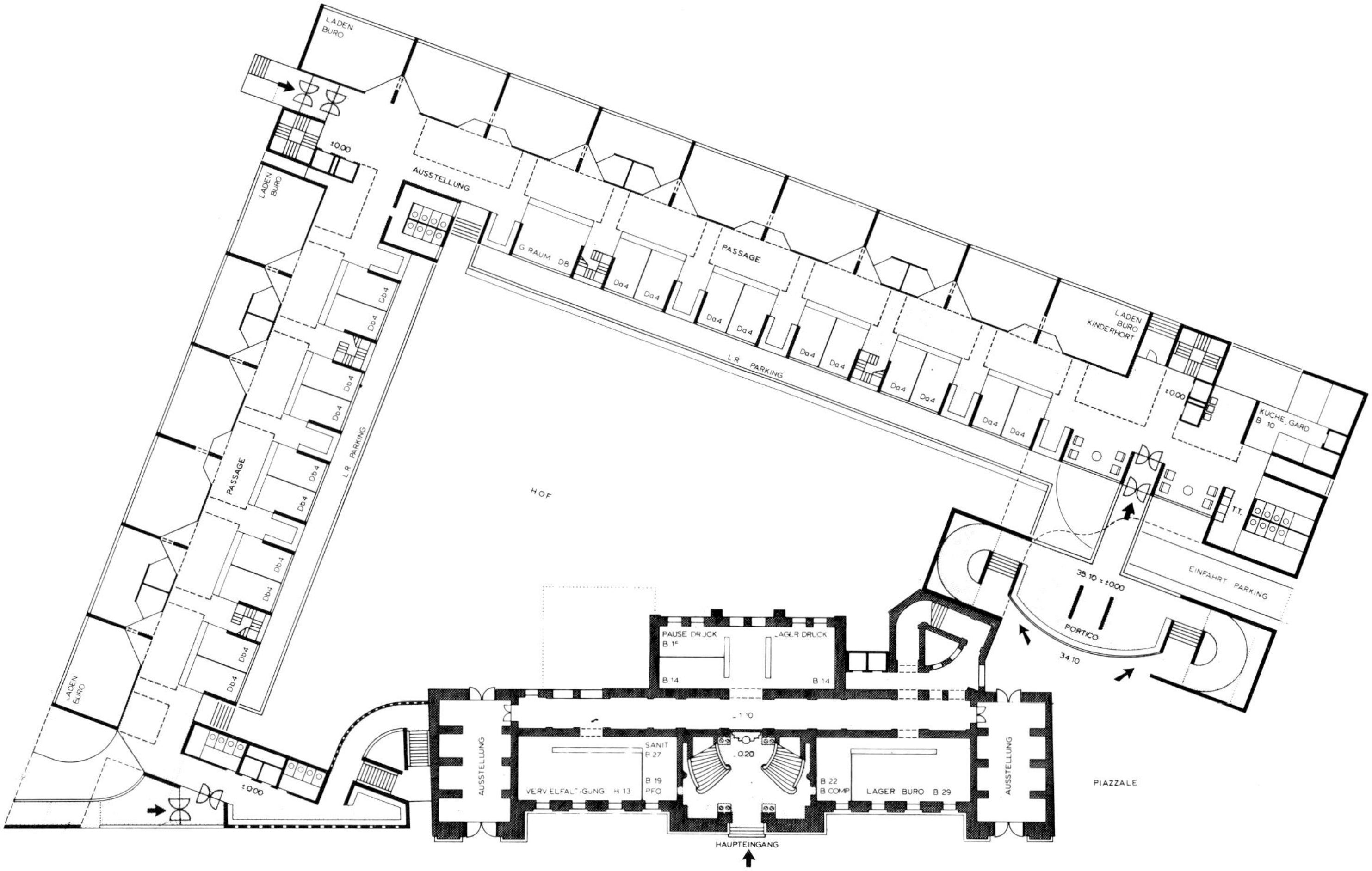

facade

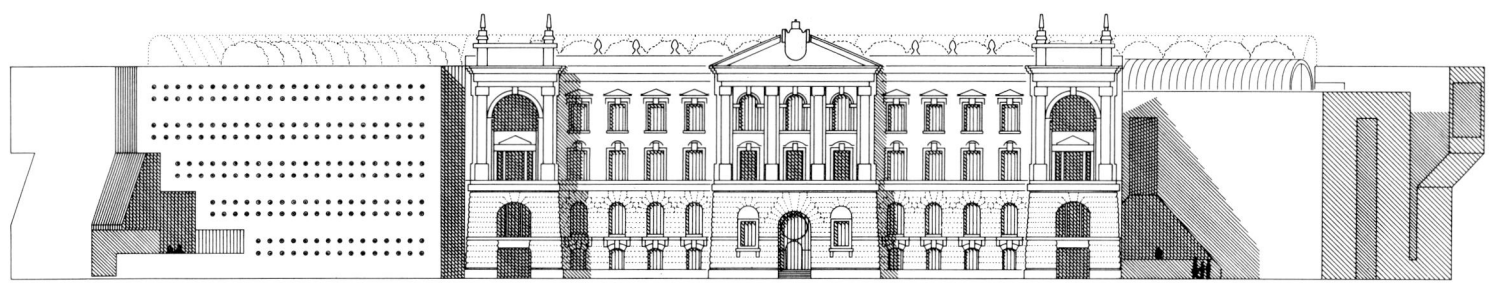

1980

Reintegration of the city center of Stuttgart, West Germany

The project entered for the competition held by the city of Stuttgart recomposes the urban fabric which was destroyed during the sixties. Two new building fronts, one on Königstrasse and the other on T. Heuss-Strasse, become the poles of a new system of pedestrian links. The present gallery on the street which runs into Schlossplatz is transformed into an art gallery for the city. It is an attempt to rectify the town planning errors committed during the last decades and an indication of what is possible.

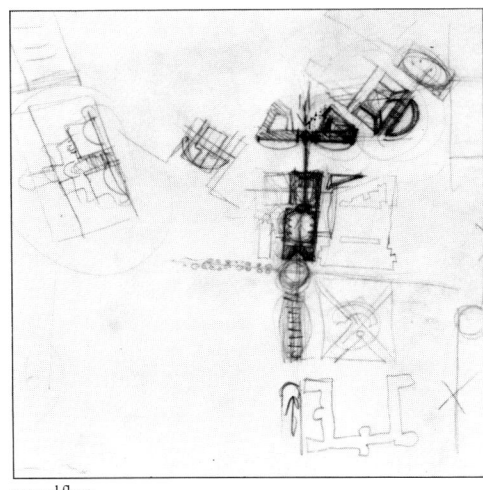

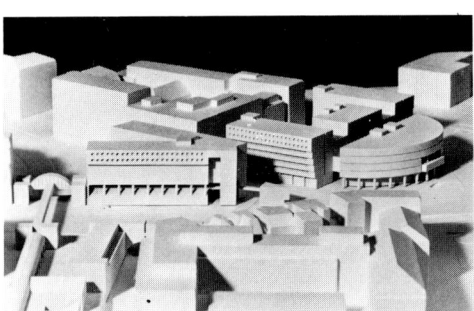

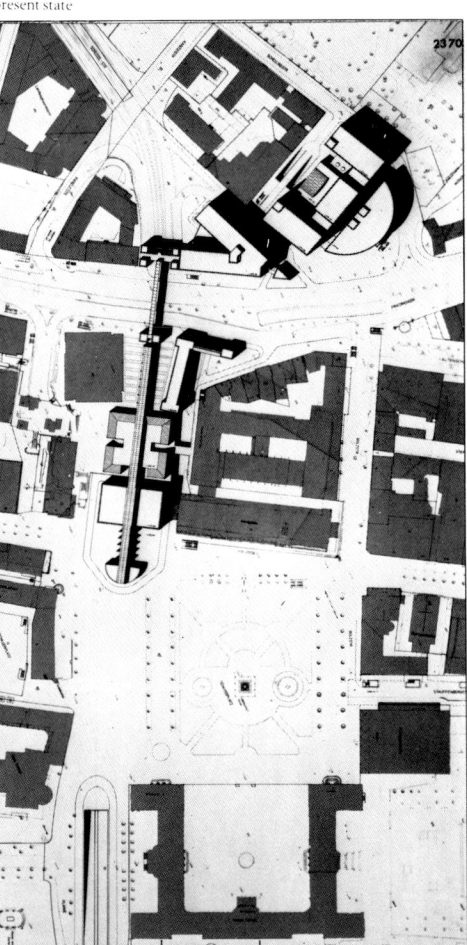

present state

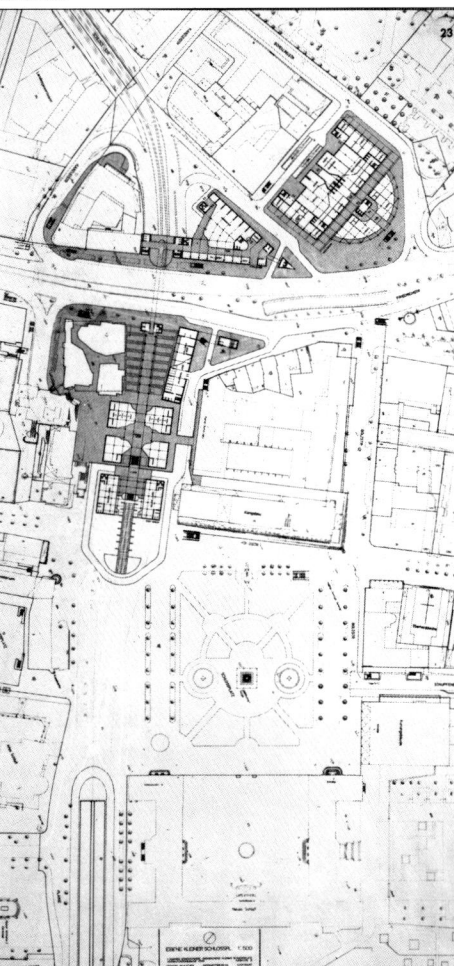

ground floor

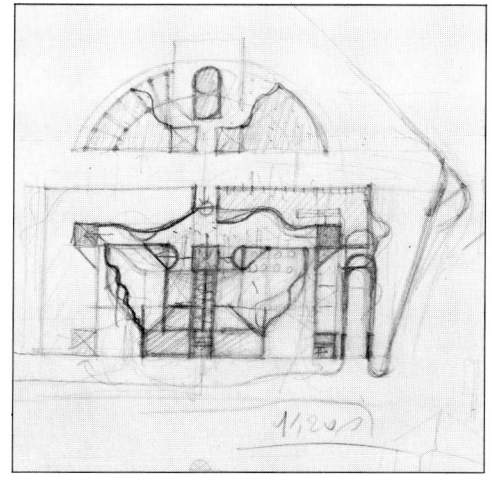
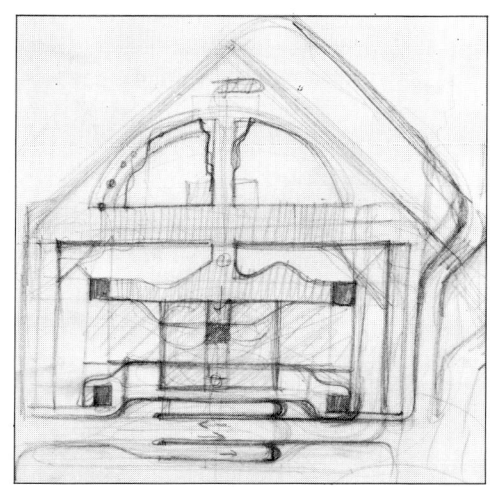

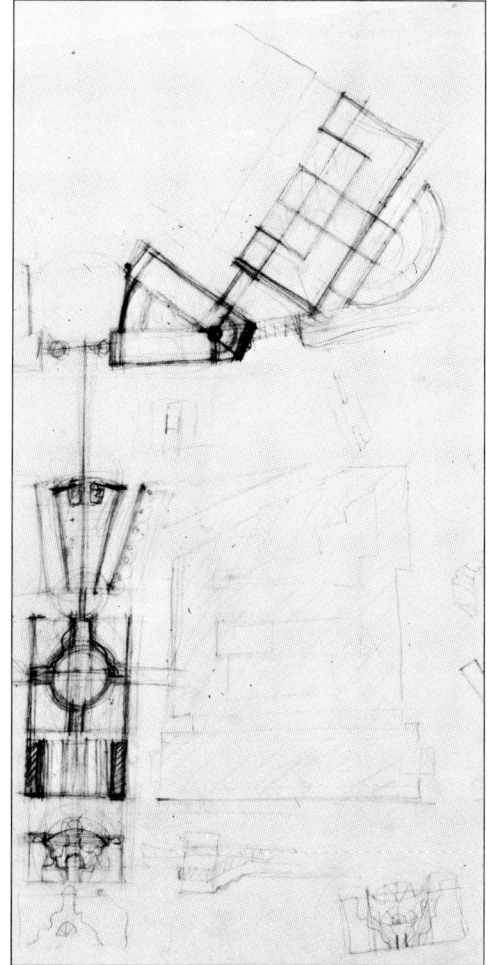

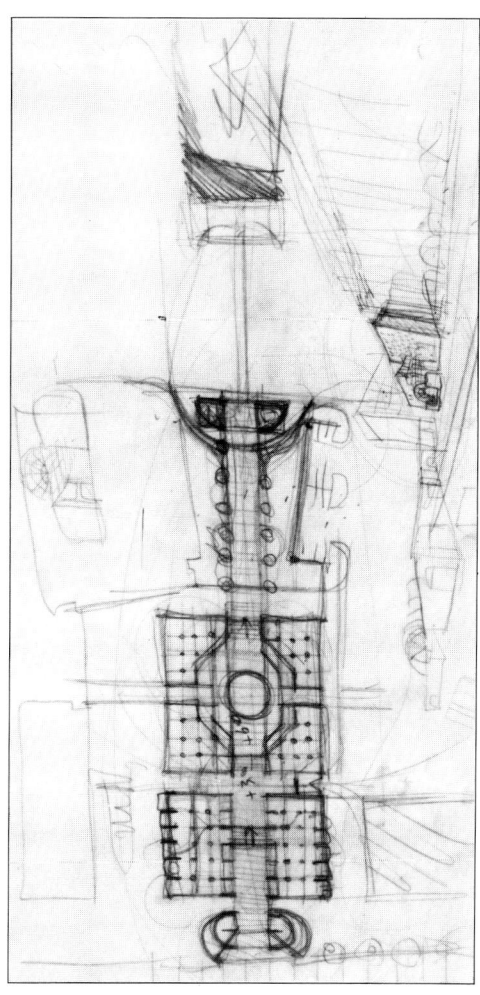

Design

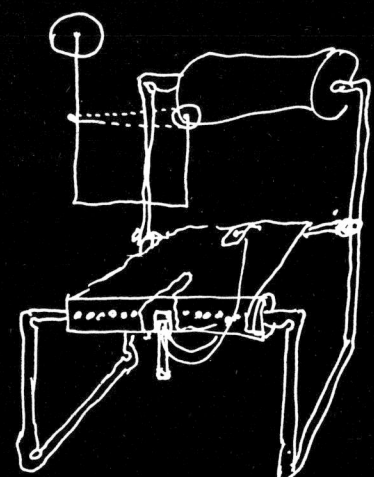

1982 **Two chairs**

Another chair? This was my first reaction on receiving an invitation from ALIAS to design one. Afterwards came curiosity, then the first attempts and the seduction that accompany design work around a theme that has constantly aroused the interest of architects and designers. In fact, we go on designing the same things. The fundamental requirements of man in the organization of space and living have not changed much.

Each time we are confronted with what has "already been done," but each time we have to start again from the beginning: a challenge and a confrontation with the blank page. Designing a chair, like designing a house, means pursuing a new image capable of representing the needs of the day, capable of responding to contemporary sensitivity, capable of suggesting new hope. To do this we are continuously redesigning ordinary objects, looking for new configurations of living space. In the act of giving expression to our aspirations we are never aware of progress but, simply, the continuity in relation to the forms and expressions that we have already made our own.

Because of this, even a chair becomes an opportunity for confrontation with our knowledge and, as always in every project, it becomes a moment of awareness and verification of our problems, our doubts and our hopes.

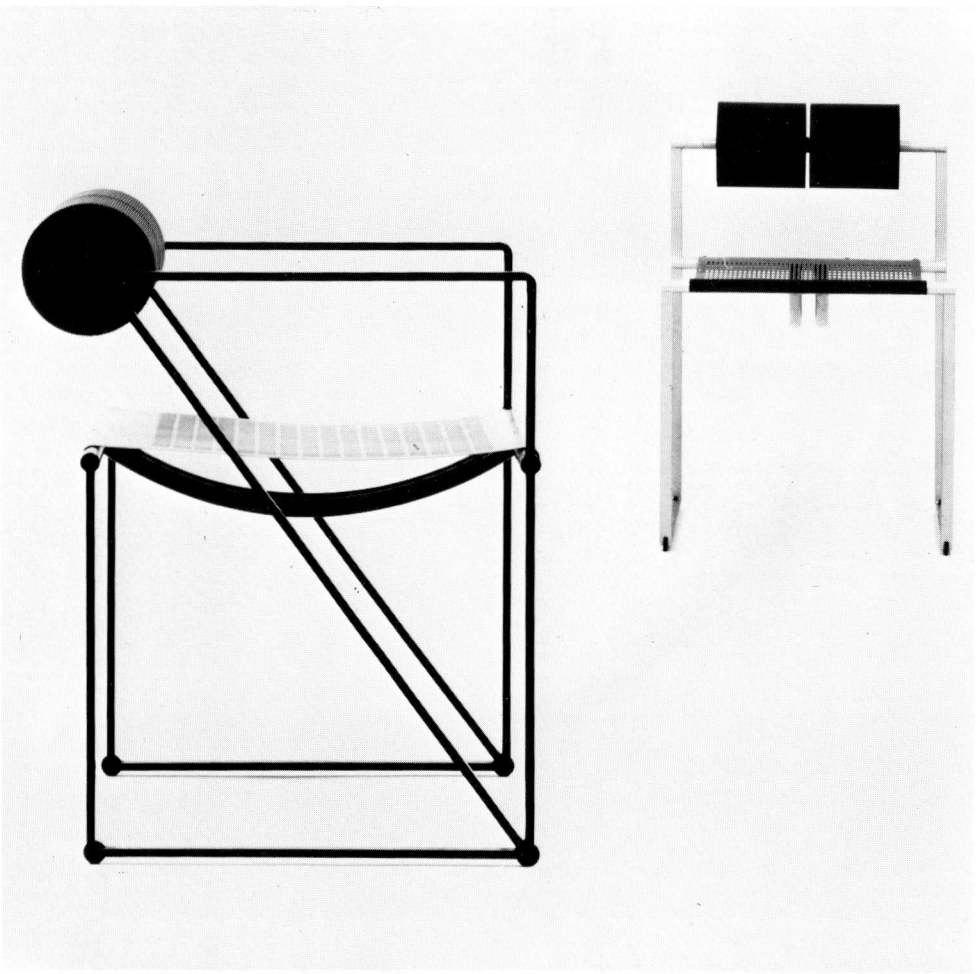

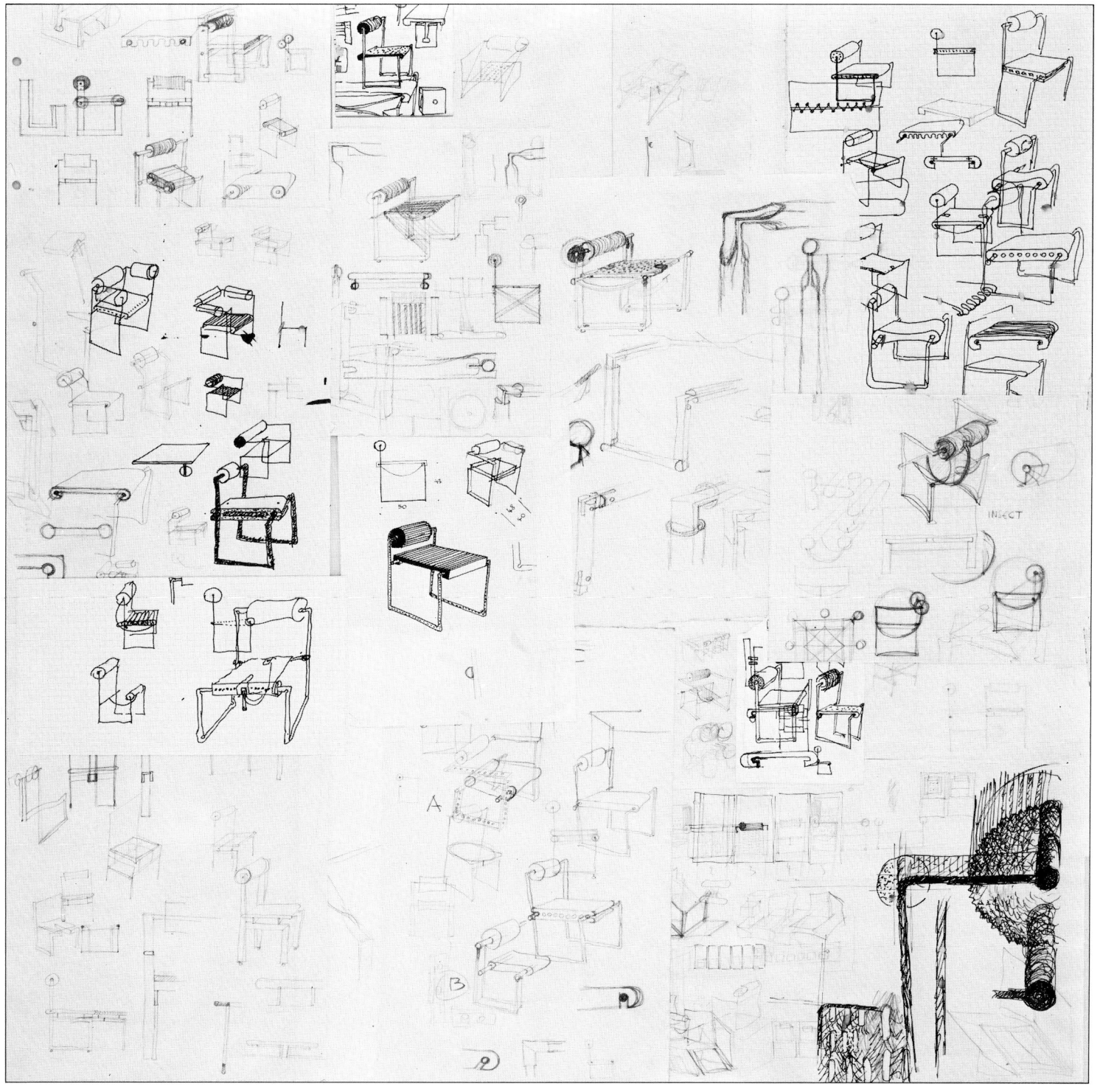

Photo by Christian Känzig

Biographical notes

1943
Mario Botta
Born in Mendrisio (Switzerland) on April 1, 1943, to a family from Genestrerio (Ticino Canton).
Primary schooling in Genestrerio.
Secondary schooling in Mendrisio.

1958-1961
Apprenticeship, as a draftsman, in the office of Carloni and Camenisch in Lugano.

1961-1964
Art school in Milan.

1964-1969
Studies at the University Institute of Architecture in Venice.

1965
Employed in the studio of Le Corbusier, at first in Venice (project for the new hospital), with Jullian de la Fuente and José Oubrerie; then at 35, Rue de Sèvres in Paris.

1969
Meeting with Louis Kahn in Venice and collaboration on the preparation of the exhibition of the plans for the new Congress Building.
Degree in architecture at the IUA in Venice, under the direction of Carlo Scarpa and Giuseppe Mazzariol.

1970
Beginning of his professional activity with the opening of a studio in Lugano.

1978
Member of the F.A.S. (Federation of Swiss Architects).

since 1979
Conferences in America and Europe.

1976, 1980, 1982
Visiting professor at the Federal Polytechnic School in Lausanne.

1982
Member of the Swiss Federal Commission for the Fine Arts.

Bibliography

1968
Bruno Alfieri, "Una casa nel Ticino," in *Lotus International*, no. 9, Venice.

1969
Giuseppe Mazzariol, "Un fiore per Le Corbusier," in *Werk*, no. 4, Zurich.

1974
Renato Pedio, "Casa unifamiliare a Riva San Vitale," in *L'architettura*, no. 223, Rome.

1975
Mario Borges, "Analyse d'une expérience," in *Werk*, no. 11, Zurich.

Martin Steinmann, *Tendenzen Neuer Architektur im Tessin*, ETH catalogue, Zurich.

1976
Hiromi Fujii, *Architecture + Urbanism*, no. 69, Tokyo.

1977
Francesco Dal Co, "Critique d'une exposition" and Bruno Reichlin, Martin Steinmann, "Critique d'une critique," in *L'architecture d'aujour d'hui*, no. 190, Paris.

Pierre von Meiss, "La maison et la ville," in *Pro Fribourg*, no. 33, Freiburg.

Maurice Culot, "Les maisons de Mario Botta," in *Archives d'architecture moderne*, no. 12, Brussels.

Lorenzo Berni, "Scuola media unica a Morbio Inferiore," in *Panorama*, no. 604, Milan.

Udo Kultermann, "Schweizerische Architektur," in *Die Architektur im 20. Jahrhundert*, Cologne.

1978
Stanislaus von Moos, "Notizen zu einigen neuen Schweizer Schulbauten," in *Werk Archithese*, nos. 13-14, Zurich.

Enrico Mantero, "Il luogo e l'edificio," in *Domus*, no. 579, Milan.

Pierre-Alain Croset, "Dorigny: la question théorique de l'architecture," in *Habitation*, no. 11, Lausanne.

Urs Graf, "Aspects de l'architecture de Mario Botta," in *Docu-Bulletin*, nos. 3-4, Blauen.

1979
Lorenzo Berni, "Progetti del concorso per l'ampliamento della stazione di Zurigo," in *Panorama*, no. 669, Milan.

Hans van Dijk, "Mario Botta — Botta's muren," in *B-NWS*, 12-28, Technische Hogeschool, Delft.

Hans van Dijk, "Tessiner Architectuur," in *Plan*, no. 5, Amsterdam.

Emilio Battisti, "L'intelligenza del mestiere," in *Lotus International*, no. 22, Milan.

Jord den Hollander, "Mario Botta: Eén van de 'Tessiner' Architecten. Dialoog tussen het bestaande en het nieuwe," in *De Architect*, no. 6, La Haye.

Kenneth Frampton, "The will to build" and Emilio Battisti, "Architectural experience," in *Mario Botta: Architecture and projects in the '70s*, Milan.

Mario Botta, "Architecture and 'environnement'," in *A + U*, no. 105, Tokyo.

Jo Coenen, "Moderne Architectur En Oude Waarden," in *Avenue*, October, Amsterdam.

Francesco Dal Co, "Discepolo di Le Corbusier che piace ai giapponesi," in *Rinascita*, no. 39, Rome.

Roberto Trevisiol, "Mario Botta," in *A Plus*, no. 61, Brussels.

Kenneth Frampton, "Mario Botta and the School of the Ticino," in *Oppositions*, no. 14, New York.

Pierluigi Nicolin, "Mario Botta: architetture e progetti negli anni '70," in *Triennale di Milano, Galleria del Disegno*, catalogue, Milan.

1980
Guglielmo Volonterio, "Fare architettura equivale a trasformare l'ambiente," in *Corriere del Ticino*, January, Lugano.

Lorenzo Berni, "Edificio per laboratori e residenze a Balerna," in *Panorama*, no. 716, Milan.

Martin Steinmann, "Mario Botta: 'Recherche patiente'," in *Archithese*, no. 1, Zurich.

Roland Dorn, "Moderne Architektur im Tessin," in *Baumeister*, no. 1, Munich.

Jean Marc Reiser, "Mario Botta," in *Charlie-Hebdo*, no. 484, Paris.

Livio Dimitriu, "Swiss Transmission and Exagerations: An Interview with Mario Botta," in *Skyline*, vol. 2, no. 8, New York.

Ulrike Jehle, "Mario Botta: Il passato come un amico," in *Werk, Bauen + Wohnen*, no. 3, Zurich.

Hans van Dijk, "Botta's muren," in *Forum*, no. 1, Amsterdam.

Mario Botta, "Une maison familiale encore!" in *Werk, Bauen + Wohnen*, no. 5, Zurich.

Charles Descloux, "Faire œuvre d'architecte c'est transformer le paysage," in *La liberté*, no. 202, Freiburg.

Elio Ostinelli, "L'architettura di Mario Botta," in *Popolo e libertà*, no. 133, Bellinzona.

Antonio Pizza, "Mario Botta: archeologo o architetto?" in *Dipartimenti architettura,* year 1, June, Venice.

Kenneth Frampton, "Architecture contemporaine," in *Encyclopaedia universalis,* Paris.

Jorge Glusberg, "La arquitectura de Mario Botta entre la historia y la memoria: el passado como amigo," in *CAYC,* Buenos Aires.

Bruno Zevi, "La poetica del muro," in *L'Espresso,* no. 38, Rome, cf. also *Cronache di Architettura,* no. 1341, Bari.

Pier Carlo Santini, "Mario Botta architetto ticinese," in *Ottagono,* no. 58, Milan.

Roberto Trevisiol, "Un château en Suisse," in *A Plus,* no. 66, Brussels.

Mario Botta, "Il disegno, il luogo e il progetto," in *Am Rand des Reissbretts: 10 Schweizer Architekten, Skizzen, Zeichnungen, Grafik, Bilder,* catalogue, Chur.

Vittorio Magnago Lampugnani, *Architektur und Städtebau des 20. Jahrhunderts,* Stuttgart.

Jürgen Joedicke, "Rationalismus," in *Architektur im Umbruch,* Stuttgart.

Kenneth Frampton, "Place, Production and Architecture: towards a critical theory of building," in *Modern Architecture: a critical history,* London.

Frank Werner, "Lieder, die man nicht erwartet," in *Bauwelt,* no. 39, Berlin.

Michael Hedgeperth, "Visit by Mario Botta," in *Archetype IV,* San Francisco.

Jean-Paul Rayon, "Mario Botta 'S'il-vous-plait, dessine-moi une maison'," in *Techniques & Architecture,* no. 332, Paris.

1981
Roberto Trevisiol, "M.B.," in *A Plus,* no. 68, January-February, Brussels.

Gruppo Specchio, "Intellectual Tradition 'Mario Botta'," in *SD Space design,* no. 3, Tokyo.

Ulrike Jehle, Bruno Reichlin, "Mario Botta... Morbio Inferiore, Tessin, Bauernhof, Umbau 1977-79," in *Architektur 1940-1980,* (Vogt-Jehle-Reichlin), Berlin.

Arnulf Lüchinger, "Mario Botta, Mittelschule in Morbio Inferiore, CH, 1972-76," in *Strukturalismus in Architektur und Städtebau,* Stuttgart.

Werner Blaser, *Architecture 70-80 in Switzerland,* Basel-Boston-Stuttgart.

Pierluigi Nicolin, "Un segno di profondità. Mario Botta: biblioteca a Lugano (Ticino)," in *Lotus International,* no. 28, Milan.

Walter Barten, "Neo-rationalistische architectuur van Botta en Grassi," in *Het Financieele Vrijdagblad,* 20 March, Amsterdam.

Bruno Odermatt, "Projektaufträge Pensione di Cura in Agra, TI," in *Schweizer Ingenieur und Architekt,* no. 14, Zurich.

Roberto Trevisiol, "Kunstgrepen volgens de wetten van de natuur," in *Knack Magazine,* no. 18, Antwerp.

Dirk Mayhöfer, "Das Streifenhaus von Ligornetto," in *Architektur & Wohnen,* fasc. 2, Hamburg.

Laura Pilarski, *Nikkey Architecture,* 2-2, Tokyo.

Maddalena Sisto, "Una scultura per abitare, le sue luci, i suoi contrasti," in *Casa Vogue,* no. 117, Milan.

Fabio Reinhart, "Frei Libre," in *As Architettura Svizzera,* 46, Pully-Lausanne.

Frank Werner, *Die vergeudete Moderne. Europäische Architekturkonzepte nach 1950, die Papier geblieben sind,* Stuttgart.

Nikolaus Pevsner, John Fleming, Hugh Honour, *Dizionario di Architettura,* Turin.

Lance Knobel, "Botta," in *AR The Architectural Review,* no. 1013, London.

Josef Paul Kleihues, "Die Neubaugebiete-Dokumente. Projekte 2," in *Internationale Bauausstellung Berlin 1984,* Berlin.

Francesco Moschini, "Mestiere come professione," in *Domus,* no. 620, Milan.

Maarten Kloos, "Architectuur van Botta overtuigend," in *De Volkskrant,* 31 March, Amsterdam.

Silvio Cassarà, "Biblioteca dei Cappuccini a Lugano," in *Parametro,* no. 99, Bologna.

Roland Hinke, "Die moderne Klassik in der Architektur," in *Das Haus,* Burda GmbH, Stuttgart.

Robert Maxwell, "Hotel/Clinic, Agra: Function & Symbol," in *International Architect,* no. 5, London.

Peter Disch, "Internationale Bauausstellung Berlin 1984 - Centro delle scienze di Berlino," and "Uno spazio per 'Guernica'," in *Rivista Tecnica,* no. 10, Bellinzona.

Jean Marc Reiser, "La maison ronde de l'architecte Mario Botta," in *Charlie Hebdo,* no. 579, Paris.

Haig Beck, "A home for Guernica's Return: Mario Botta's Competition Design," in *International Architect,* no. 6, London.

Martin Dominguez, "Une soirée à Morbio," in *Quadernos,* no. 147, Barcelona.

Mario Botta, "Ein Raum für Gernika," in *Werk, Bauen + Wohnen,* no. 11, Zurich.

1982
Luciana Caglio, "Mario Botta: 'L'architettura

può diventare un'alleata del territorio'," in *Azione,* 28 January, Lugano.

György Kévés, "Mario Botta," in *Mü Vészet,* Budapest.

Mario Botta, "L'albero come eccezione," in *Lotus International,* no. 31, Milan.

Stefano Casciani, "La casa rotonda," in *Domus,* no. 626, Milan.

Bruno Zevi, "Sua maestà il paesaggio," in *L'Espresso,* no. 9, Rome.

Paolo Portoghesi, "Guernica tolto a Guernica?," in *Europeo,* no. 13, Milan.

Mario Botta, "Casa a Stabio," in *Rivista Tecnica,* no. 2, Bellinzona.

Gudrun Rapasch, "Wohn-Turm über Luganer See," in *Das Haus,* Stuttgart.

Pierluigi Nicolin, "Notes on the House at Stabio (1981) and the House at Pregassona (1979)," in *Ga Global Architecture Houses 10,* Tokyo.

Edoardo Sanguineti, Alberto Sartoris, Pierluigi Nicolin, Rob Krier, Reiser, Roberto Trevisiol, *Mario Botta - La casa rotonda,* Milan.

François Chaslin, "Théâtres dans la ville," in *Architecture,* no. 36, Paris.

Frank Werner, "Gegenwarts-Architektur" and Mario Botta, "Gernika," in *Vergangenheit Gegenwart Zukunft,* catalogue, Stuttgart.

Emile Duhart Echeverria, "Tessin une tradition moderne," in *Décoration Internationale,* no. 52, Paris.

Peter Arnell, "Mario Botta: Trans-Alpine Rationalist," in *Architectural Record,* June.

Rita Cirio, debate between Paolo Portoghesi and Mario Botta, "Architetto, che stai architettando?," in *L'Espresso,* nos. 27-28, Rome.

Loyd Grossman, "Milan's Post-Modern Masters," in *Harpers & Queen,* May, London.

Luciano Rubino, "Natura e volumi bloccati," in *Tuttoville,* no. 72, Milan.

Livio Dimitriu, "Transfigurer of geometry," in *Progressive Architecture,* June, Stamford.

Pierre-Alain Croset, "Una casa da feudatari," in *Casabella,* no. 482, Milan.

Béatrix de l'Aulnoit, "Des architectes à visiter: Vivre au milieu du pré," in *Cosmopolitan,* no. 106, Paris.

Pierluigi Nicolin, "La firma dell'architetto, oppure: l'uomo propone l'architetto dispone," in *Interni,* no. 323, Milan.

Pierre-Alain Croset, "Mario Botta - La Banca dello Stato di Friburgo," in *Casabella,* no. 484, Milan.